Declutter Your Home

—————— ❧❦❦❧ ——————

The Ultimate Guide to Simplify and Organize Your Home

Chloe S

or abuse of any policies, processes, or directions contained within is the solitary and utter responsibility of the recipient reader. Under no circumstances will any legal liability or blame be held against the publisher for any reparation, damages, or monetary loss due to the information herein, either directly or indirectly.

Respective authors own all copyrights not held by the publisher.

The information herein is offered for informational purposes solely and is universal as so. The presentation of the information is without a contract or any guarantee assurance.

The trademarks that are used are without any consent, and the publication of the trademark is without permission or backing by the trademark owner. All trademarks and brands within this book are for clarifying purposes only and are the owned by the owners themselves, not affiliated with this document.

Table of Contents

Introduction

I want to thank you and congratulate you for purchasing the book, *"Declutter Your Home."*

This book contains *proven* steps and painless strategies about how to declutter your home.

Have you ever imagined how much junk you have lying around the house? What happened that time when a friend called you and said she'd drop by in a *few minutes?* Yikes! You immediately went into a panic, as you glanced at the shelves in your wall unit and noticed all the dust. Of course, you didn't have time to pick up very little knick-knack and dust underneath. What's more, you have a wealth of appliances occupying space on your kitchen counters because there's no more room in the cabinets to store them. There's barely enough space to prepare a little snack for your guest! Besides, everybody *always goes into the kitchen.* And yours is a horror show! *(Gasp!)*

Well, it is sad that most of us even have more than a little. Before you became enlightened, you barely noticed the clutter anymore. It is as if it becomes "friendly clutter." The marketing mavens of the world have surreptitiously misled people into believing that material things can help fill their human needs for self-esteem and social status. At this point, you have come to realize that all of that clutter is just STUFF! According to polls conducted by the National Association of Professional Organizers, over 65 % of American people often have the feeling that their house is disorganized and cluttered. So, you aren't alone. Many others are like you. What the others may not know is the fact that clutter accumulation in the house is very detrimental to human health. In many instances, it is clutter that stirs up stress. You've reached that point now, haven't you? Rather than get out your frustrations at the gym, why not harness your energy toward a more productive task?

Because you have picked up this book, you have already come to the understanding that living a simple and uncluttered life is very attractive. Can you imagine how terrific it would feel if you could tell any unexpected guest "Oh, sure...come on over?" Can you imagine yourself feeling delighted about your visitor, rather than rush about stressed out about the condition of your house! You want your house to be a home, not a multi-room storage locker.

To make your "house makeover" permanent, it is crucial to debunk the myths promulgated by that notorious army of greedy marketing mavens.

Although your clutter only consists of material things, letting go isn't easy – believe it or not. Therefore, it is crucial to understand the psychological reasons for your attachment to your stuff. Once you are freed from all those items holding you back, you will undergo a personal transformation. Is it possible the decluttering can have such a grandiose outcome? Yes, it is! It is a feeling of exhilarated freedom and mental tranquility.

Thank you for purchasing this book. You will benefit from it!

Chapter 1:

Congratulations!

I sn't that what is said when people graduate and embark on the journey toward a bright and prosperous future? What does that have to do with decluttering your home? A great deal. Decluttering is not merely a long and weary exercise meant to help you divest yourself of the unnecessary, unwanted and useless. It is a major step in *Self-Transformation!*

In a study by the *Association of Consumer Research*, Aaron Ahuvia and Nancy Wong proved that there is a negative relationship between life satisfaction and materialism. In fact, they took it one step further through the administration of standardized tests when results showed that "...high aspirations for income is <u>negatively</u> associated with life satisfaction." That is what is promulgated worldwide. Likewise, the clarion call of advertisers tells you that ownership is a sign of success, riches, and happiness. Clinical studies have proven that this is not true.

What!? Even wealth and the symbols of wealth won't deliver self-satisfaction?

Things, including money, are unrewarding in and of themselves.

Chapter 2:

Debunking the Clutter Myths

Your Personal Revelation

In your latest trip around your house, you noted all the clutter you've amassed over the years. It didn't help you feel satisfied; it led to stress. Did you feel overwhelmed too? Consider this real-life tale:

Sandi's Paths

Sandi's two friends from graduate school, Jenny, and Phil lived miles away from Sandi. One day, they were going to be in the area and thought they might stop by and visit her. Sandi, who had been feeling depressed welcomed the visit and invited them over.

With happy anticipation, they rang her bell.

Sandi met them with a very warm greeting and ushered them inside. Jenny and Phil were led up the hallway and into the living room. Much to their astonishment, the living room was full of boxes, and there were additional unpackaged items stacked up in piles. Gingerly, the visitors were led on paths around the stacks and directed toward the kitchen. It was the <u>only place</u> where there were three unoccupied chairs!

Furtively, Jenny and Phil exchanged worried glances. Feeling the need to rationalize her "collection," Sandi explained that she was reorganizing her things. Evidence of dust on the multitude of boxes told the tale that Sandi was procrastinating and sidetracking her worthy goal. She was no doubt feeling overwhelmed and became stuck in a rut, paralyzed by her negative emotions.

As you noted all the clutter in your home, did you have visions of a future like that? No doubt, you may have. That is why you're breaking into a new direction in life. Although it might be a tad frightening, you are courageously taking up the gauntlet to combat the problem head-on.

Shedding the Old Myths

Philosophers and teachers throughout time have traditionally rejected the lure of greed and materialism. With the current 21st century movement toward minimalism, people have started eschewing the myths that there would be a psychological benefit to an accumulation of things. Among the false beliefs are:

- **Myth 1:** Self-Esteem can be attained through possessions.

- **Myth 2:** The esteem of others can be secured through ownership.

- **Myth 3:** Life is more convenient and easier if you conform to societal expectations.

- **Myth 4:** Security in oneself can be reinforced through materialism.

- **Myth 5:** Sentimental attachments give one a sense of emotional wellness.

Myth 1: Self-Esteem Can Be Attained through Possessions

In 1995, an elderly man was once interred along with his beloved Corvette. It was said of him that he "wanted to go out in style." Rather than being remembered for his winning personality, his caring, or his virtue, his friends, and others read his obituary and thought of him as the guy who was buried in his car!

As you watch TV or surf the Internet, you are pummeled with commercials and ads. When you walk through a large "big box" store, the glass windows are frightfully obscured with immense signs heralding "lower" prices or announcing specials. Once inside, you are bombarded with signs and sometimes even flashing lights.

Standing displays block large portions of the aisles, which children knock over periodically.

There is, of course, one purpose to this barrage. To sell. Have you ever noticed what the sales profession calls their pitch? The "Call to Action." To achieve that, mighty promises are made. Most have to do with your self-image. You will be smarter than all the rest if you buy thus-and-so. You will feel better once you are the "proud owner" of a product. You will look better if you use this or that...terrific! Furthermore, the sales pitch adds: "Do it *Now!*" "Now" is a keyword of advertising. "Be the first to own..." is another catchphrase.

Today, there is such an emphasis on possessions and ownership that – indeed – people have been misled into considering objects necessary for their self-esteem. This can happen very easily, and it is human nature.

In his theory of motivation, the noted psychologist, Abraham Maslow, has indicated that every human being has set of needs. Self-esteem and the esteem of others are seen as some of the higher-level needs. One needs to find fulfillment in his or her esteem needs, and that will serve as a distinct motivation to grow as a person. What the advertisers have done is to imply that the possession of "stuff" will help you meet those needs and consider yourself a worthy person. That is quite a tall order for a material object. One can also realize a sense of self-fulfillment in the accumulation of things, so they say.

Have you ever noticed how huge corporations attempt to outdo the other? They try to buy out other companies, merge the two, or simply raid the lesser corporation for its monetary worth alone. Owners of such corporations do battle with each other also so that they can be perceived as the epitome in their respective fields. Don't you love it when billionaires fight?

Brief Exercise:

1. Make a list of all your positive qualities.

2. Made a list of all your negative characteristics.

3. Try to even out the list. That is, note that you put down more negative traits than positive ones. Spend some time thinking about your positive characteristics and list them.

4. Ask yourself the following question: Will owning that item or items help me feel better as a person?

5. Reflect on this quote from "The Little Prince" by Antoine de Saint-Exupery: "It is only with the heart that one can see rightly. What is essential is invisible to the eye."

<u>Preliminary Solution:</u>

Scribble a drawing of one room in your house. Notice how you left all the clutter out. No one wants to put their clutter on display, so you mentally eliminated it. Scan that room again noticing how it looks. Now create a visual picture of how you would *like* the room to look. Create a décor in your mind that you would want without the clutter. Once you've created that visual image, keep it in your mind as you begin the process of decluttering. Visual imagery is a powerful motivator.

Myth 2: The Esteem of Others Can Be Secured through Ownership

Today, people are often admired based on how many things they own. Surely, you've heard people utter with great majesty: "Oh! *I* have one of those!" Besides, take a look at written articles about achieving success. Virtually all of them indicate how many things the successful person owns. Because of that, you are expected to admire and respect them. Many fall into that trap.

In actuality, people read stories about successful entrepreneurs because they want to compete with them not have all the things they have. If that entrepreneur is successful, all you need do is mimic their formulas, and you too can be as rich, as happy, and as successful as they are. Concerning celebrities, the film director, Martin Scorsese said, "You get to love them. They don't know you. But you love them. But you love, I think, is what you imagine they are...they represent a dream. You lose yourself in these people." However, take a closer look. Those celebrities who have a truly unique style are admired because of their skills and personalities, not because of their wealth or how many things they own.

1. The Call to Conformity

   In modern society, the "Tyrants of Conformity" parade tempting images before you with the implication – either overt or implied – that you must act, dress, look, and own things to gain the esteem of others. Furthermore, you have been inculcated with the notion that ownership is necessary to reach a certain status in society. For example, you might hear someone say in astonishment: "What? You don't have the latest iPhone?" "Don't you have a riding lawnmower yet?"

You are "supposed" to have a laptop, a cell phone, a flat screen TV, and, also, be trim and fit, muscular, wear a lot of stylish clothes, have a lot of hair, maintain certain hairstyles, and spend your morning routines trying to look like a model. *Why? So people will like you!* In contradiction to the call to conformity, have you ever noticed that the visual images advertised show home interiors with NO electronic gadgets strewn about here and there? Obviously, there is something inherently wrong with the belief that ownership makes the person.

There are odd behaviors, also, that you are expected to follow. When you travel the aisles in a grocery store, somehow, you are expected to speak in subdued tones. Anyone deviating will attract undue attention. (Children love to do that, don't they?) If you work in a corporate office, you are supposed to wear skimpy dresses or slim, trim suits – a different one each day of the week. Your wardrobe costs a fortune. If you don't adhere to the tenets of conformity, the prevailing attitude is that you won't be liked. There are a countless number of successful entrepreneurs who don't conform. They look like ordinary people without a lot of trappings and paraphernalia. That's what makes them interesting. They are not conformists; they are unique.

2. The False Goal of Conformity

For years, you have been misled to believe that conformist behavior leads to the respect and esteem of others. To meet your objectives in life, you *simply* must follow the precepts of practices according to the overlords of society. Really?

The real outcome of conformity is vastly different than the belief that you will attain the esteem of others. As you look upon a crowd of conformists, you don't see any significant differences. No one stands out. Do you want to be a nameless face in a sea of other nameless faces? Of course not!

3. Conformity ≠ Esteem of Others. So, how do you achieve the esteem of others? You don't! The esteem of others is not achieved. It is freely given, and you cannot control it. Some say that you "earn" the esteem of others. That belief is faulty. It is not up to you to "earn" or "strive" toward the esteem of others. It is a human failing to try to attain the attention of others. The esteem of others flows from who you are, and not what you own. There once was a character who appeared in cartoons during the 1930s. He famously said: "I am what I am and that's all that I am. I'm Popeye, the sailor man."

4. Irrational Beliefs

   People who crave the esteem of others subscribe to the code that it is necessary the everyone approves of them. They believe that unhappiness is caused by someone or something outside of oneself. Not to be undone, others believe that every unhappy event that befalls them is caused by themselves. Those folks are the "It's my fault" mob. You've seen that most vividly in teenagers. An unhappy girl feels that owning designer jeans and designer bags will make everyone like her more. Perhaps she is liked but doesn't even know it. It is also true that no one is liked by virtually everyone!

Myth 3: Life Is More Convenient and Easier If You Conform to Societal Expectations

Many commercials and ads display electronic devices that supposedly take the place of many other devices. Your cell phone now seems to do everything for you except put gas in your car! Devices pop up in your kitchen or living room that take commands. The sales pitch crows that you no longer need a lot of devices now – each for a specific purpose – all you need now is one device can do everything! The word *convenient* is added to all the jingles! How many times have you heard someone cry out in frustration: "Where is _____? *My whole life is in that _____!*" Wow! Your life is locked up in a memory chip! How convenient is that? "No, wait!" the advertisers say, "Now we have a device that tells you where your other device is!" So, now you have one device with everything on it, and a second device that tells you where it is! Each device comes with adapter cables or plugs for recharging. Then there's an extra cable in case you want to plug anything into your cigarette lighter. Now, you have up to five pieces of clutter!

Not to be outdone, clever entrepreneurs have designed containers in which to keep your things. It's a "convenient" way to avoid decluttering too!

While some people think that the best option is to get containers in which to pack these things, the truth is that it helps you avoid the most painful thing of all! Getting rid of the clutter. You can easily stack up containers on the top of your closet shelf until they reach the ceiling, but you'll have to deal with the items inside someday. The easiest way to get rid of this stuff is to make it a game to get rid of at least ten things each day. This means that, if you have emotional attachments to things but know you don't have room to store them, you can find creative ways to preserve memories without necessarily keeping all the items. Some of the things that create clutter include photos, souvenirs, and albums –

digital and otherwise. Other targets include small appliances and utensils you no longer use, old makeup kits, excess bedding, and vestiges from old technologies such as DVDs, cassettes, and CDs among others.

The things that we love to keep are not self-sufficient! Those things require that you dust them, care for them, maintain them, pack, unpack and rearrange them. They need more attention than pets! If their things that you don't need, spending your time and effort cleaning them is a waste. Hard as it is to let go of things you've spent money on, it's even harder to waste energy and time storing stuff that you don't care about. Most of the time you run out of places to store everything.

The truth of the matter is that convenience doesn't justify keeping clutter in the house. Therefore, if what you have is junk, unnecessary duplicates, tattered or even broken items, you have to get rid of them.

The Legend of King Midas

In the sixth century, the legend of King Midas was born. He was the King of Phrygia in Asia Minor. He loved his luxury, and most of all loved gold. King Midas loved his things, but especially gold – lots of it. Soon he was noted, not for who he was as a person, but for his wealth. When Dionysius, the god of wine visited him, he offered Midas a wish. Because gold attracted so many powerful and influential people, Midas wished that everything he touched would turn into gold. Predictably, his food and drink turned into gold. Even his beloved daughter was converted into a golden statue. The fate of craving for the esteem of others is starvation, the ultimate loss of any chance to obtain the esteem of others.

According to Tsang et al. in the journal *Personality and Individual Differences*, "Materialism has been consistently related to lower levels of life satisfaction." In the years of the latter twentieth century and the twenty-first century, materialism has come to symbolize a social category. You have all heard the phrases: the "have's" and the "have-not's." This focus on ownership increases paranoid fears ("I might get robbed!) That certainly isn't satisfying. Take a look at poor Sadie's story:

Sadie's Little House

Sadie lived in a quaint little brick house in the country. She had many precious items on the multitudinous shelves there – golden figurines, tea sets of pure silver, ancient gold coins, Japanese Netsuke figurines, and the like. She enjoyed the adulation of neighbors and reveled in taking them on trips to her home, which she called a "museum." Her life was easy and convenient. Sadie had two children, who moved out and had their own families. They lived quite a distance from Sadie, as they weren't very fond of her. After all, they spent most of their young years forbidden to "touch" any of her precious things. As she grew older, the children who had children of their own did occasionally visit but had a secret agenda. They were hoping to ascertain what was in Sadie's will.

When Sadie died, her children and grandchildren dutifully attended the funeral. Her son arrived in a pickup truck, and her daughter had a U-Haul. Toward the end of the funeral, Sadie's son left in his truck with his family. He was followed shortly after that by Sadie's daughter.

On the street in front of Sadie's house, her son parked and began raiding the house. So did her daughter. In the middle of the street, a heated argument broke out between them. "But Mom promised me her rings and gold jewelry!" squealed her daughter. Then her brother bellowed: "I'm the first-born and am entitled to whatever I want!"

In the meantime, the grandchildren ran in and out of the house toting as many objects as they could carry. A crowd gathered, and the police were called to quell the disturbance.

The above is a true story, including the truck, the U-Haul, and trained grandchildren! Perhaps you have heard other stories like that too.

Unfortunately, poor Sadie felt that others would only care about her if she could entertain them with her many precious things. People will like you for who you are as a person.

 Preliminary Solution (more to follow):

When you reflect on someone you like, ask yourself if the many conveniences their goods provided are the foundation for your fondness. When you think of someone you dislike, ask yourself if the lack of convenience in their lifestyle is the foundation for your negative feelings. The answer is a resounding "No!"

Now, when you think about someone who has an expensive foreign car with a chauffeur and lives in what is dubbed a "mini-mansion," do you think about their personalities? No! Years from now, if someone asks you about that person with expensive items and an easy life, you nearly always say: "Oh! He had a _____ and life was so much easier for him." One hounding follow-up question remains: "Does the convenience of ownership mean he or she is esteemed?"

It is usually the person who has a *less* convenient life who is more admired.

Myth 4: Security in Oneself can be Reinforced through Materialism.

According to some of the ancient philosophies, "materialism" is a firm conviction that nothing exists except matter and its movements. Many people you know go from one day to the next in a humdrum pace to maintain their standard of living, raise families, and simply survive. Since the Industrial Revolution, one's job has been the foundation for survival. It has become the motivation to work. In some cultures, citizens live to work, rather than work to live. The worship of the ever-growing desire for higher-paying jobs has been nominated as one's goal in life. According to M. L. Richins et al., "An important cause of increasing work and declining leisure among people is their materialistic values."

When you see your baby, you marvel at the wonder and awe he demonstrates toward others and the environment. When he looks out the window, he is wide-eyed when he sees a bird land on a branch outside. When you make a funny face, he giggles. When you pick him up and cuddle him, he feels delighted. When you feed him, he is content and happy. Family and friends give him toys, which he touches and caresses. However, he never asks for more. He loves you, and you cannot help but respond with love. Love is not material, yet it is what he needs most to survive.

As your child grows, however, suddenly he feels the need for things. Objects such as cell phones, computer tablets, video and music-related devices tend to bring him a sense of security. Meals, a warm house, and clothing are no longer sufficient. By the time your children reach adolescence, their rooms are so cluttered with objects that there's barely little space left for sleeping! You used to say "He outgrew his clothes." Now you can say, "His room outgrew him!"

In the process of self-examination, you discover that security seems to have become associated, not only with the necessities of physical survival but also with *things*.

What happened?

According to Hyunji Kim et al., this is called "personal relative deprivation." That means that people assess their feelings of a security relative to others. The most astounding result of Kim's five studies showed that absolute household income and ownership had much more to do with the **desire** for financial success and power than security. There is an undercurrent of fear involved in detaching yourself from things you feel are needed to give you a sense of security. Some possessions, of course, are necessary for human survival and to provide a sense of physical security. However, things will never provide psychological security. That kind of security comes from within.

Your self-image and sense of security within yourself depends on you, not what you own. Your esteem needs are fulfilled by your behaviors.

Your need for love relies on others. You need to reach a level of self-actualization is accomplished through your values and attitudes. It takes great courage to move ahead in life when the most important elements of life depend upon your personality and spirit, not the material possessions you have.

Preliminary Solution (more to follow):

Mentally create this mindset – Freedom!

The sooner you get started on detaching yourself from material possessions, the sooner you will realize that there are other priorities such as placing more importance on experiences. At this point, you will have a strong sense of lightness. You will feel more secure knowing that you are more valuable than your things. It is like putting down all the load that you have been carrying for a very long time. You can channel your energy into people, family, friends, and experiences. Imagine scenes of enjoyment. Picture meaningful interactions with people you care about.

Myth 5: Sentimental Attachments Give One a Sense of Emotional Wellness

Yes! The photos. Is your cell phone exploding with them? Has anybody ever told you they want to show you a photo? Then they pick up their cell phone and flick through image after image until they find it. (In the meantime, you check your watch.) Before the cell phones, there were the notorious photo albums. Every trip you ever took, every family event, every attractive scene which looks like the work of a professional photographer is in those albums. What about the gifts? When Millie was seventy-years-old, she had lovely presents that her family and friends gave her on the holidays throughout the years. If someone remarked about her old jacket, Millie would surprisingly comment: "Oh, that's Sue's jacket." Well, it wasn't "Sue's jacket" at all; it was the jacket Sue gave her many moons ago! Millie couldn't bear to part with it because Sue was her favorite niece. Whenever she took new visitors for a little house tour, she always identified many of her possessions by the names of the people who gave them to her. "Aunt Camille's candy dish...Larry's vase...Maggie's chime clock..." Of course, that left visitors very puzzled.

In your heart of hearts, do you silently do that too? Is it from a fear of forgetting the past that creates the need to keep so many things? What is truly important from your past is how others have affected you and how you affect them. It is pleasant to reflect upon the warmth others have shared with you. Most of the people you have met have changed you in some way. It is what is in your heart and your memory that you cherish. It does not depend upon "reminder objects."

Many cultures and even religions throughout the centuries have placed value on the memories of their ancestors from the last generation. In Old Japan, they remembered their parents by carving soapstone statuettes of them. The people didn't save any other mementos. No doubt, you have the seen the simplistic style of their homes – free from clutter and trappings.

Preliminary Solution (more to follow):

The trick to becoming clutter-free is to think of it as a mental or spiritual exercise in which you shed the shackles of becoming a slave to your memories and the STUFF that those mementos entail. The sentiment exists in memory. The physical thing once enjoyed, is no longer relevant. Your past is derived from the experience of the warmth and caring of others and the love you have for them. Love is not a physical thing.

Chapter 3:

How to Start Decluttering

The most challenging thing of all is the start. What makes that so difficult is the feeling of being overwhelmed. That's normal. However, do you wait for the ideal time? The ideal time is *now*.

A series of transitions characterize every life. Decluttering represents a transition from what you were to what you will become. Transitional periods are unsettling. Your greatest need during this time is to find simple and painless ways to put things in the right order even in the most unfavorable conditions. The best way to do this is to pay close attention to the clutter that causes you the most frustration.

Initial exercise #1: Clutter Patrol!

1. *In your home, go from one room to the other.*

2. *Select the room that has the least amount of clutter.*

3. *Make a note of the time.*

4. *Put all objects that do not belong in that room back into their rightful places. Don't examine or scrutinize the contents of drawers or closets. That comes later in the process.*

5. *Move into the next least cluttered room. Do the same.*

6. *Continue to move from one room to the next, putting your stuff into the proper rooms. There will still be clutter leftover.*

7. *Take a look at your watch and make a note of how long this exercise took you. That will give you an idea of how serious your situation is.*

8. *Accept the fact that this is going to involve work...unpaid work! Make a firm commitment to pursue the task until you are finished.*

Initial Exercise #2: A Family Affair

1. *Schedule a family meeting.*

2. *Announce that you intend to embark on the project of decluttering your home, and indicate that it will continue for quite some time.*

3. *Children from the age of ten and up wonder if that means you will be entering their rooms. Inform them that you will. If they offer many objections, enlist their help and teach them the method that you will adopt. Have them start with their rooms. Many will not keep up this activity, and you may need to remind them. Do so gently. If they don't cooperate with your efforts, enter their rooms and*

start with your chosen method. When you start, speak to them and start asking questions about the usefulness of one or two items. Watch! They will show up in a grand hurry, and you can thus get their help.

4. Likewise, enlist the support of your spouse. You may have to cite certain trouble spots which he/she has left messy and cluttered. Tell your spouse that you don't want to decide upon which items to discard without his or her input.

Schedule and Organize

The first impediment to the deliberate act of decluttering your home is the emotional static it will create. Review the prior chapter and reflect upon the roots of materialism. Note that materialism is deleterious to your mental health and sense of well-being. Virtually all the clinical studies have confirmed that. The term "scheduling" seems innocuous enough, but it's a disciplinary practice. It's the first step. In the beginning, you may feel the need to make micro-movements. The micro-movements are composed of short sessions that can last up to 5 minutes each. You can also choose to declutter in 15-minute sessions or an hour a day. If it is possible, considering your work plan and effort, you might be able to do this as a 3-5 days marathon activity. Finally, another option is to choose to declutter each day of the week throughout the year. Believe it or not, most people increase their decluttering periods with time. You see, as they become more overwhelmed by the volume of stuff they've collected, it increases their motivation to continue. The growing frustration with the accumulation of things also serves as an incentive to complete this task quickly.

Designate a Purpose for Each Room

Every room should convey and mood. You may have some larger rooms that serve dual purposes, and you can separate one area from the other. For instance, you can designate the den as the place in which you would love to sit with your family and watch movies, television, chat, have fun and conduct recreational activities. Therefore, the proper mood to exude there is that of comfort and connection. In the laundry room, you might want to ensure that it is organized in such a manner to avoid any pile ups. The bathroom can have a spa-like surrounding to give a sweet, luxurious feeling. The master bedroom can have a romantic feel to it and yet be comfortable at the same time. Whichever room you are examining, ensure that you plan to organize it based on the function each room serves and the 'feel' you would like the room to have! That will help you decide to move related ancillary items from one room into the other. If you are going to study or read, you will need a comfortable chair or maybe a recliner, tall and small lamps, side tables (for snacks), and shelving for books. Perhaps your living room wall unit is crammed full of knick-knacks. If you plan on using that room a lot, your laptop might be appropriate to store on one of the shelves rather than knick-knacks. Why put it on the end table in your bedroom? Or carry it around with you. After all, you don't have to use your laptop in bed or at the dinner table. The Internet and your apps will survive without you! That way you can interact with your family in the dining room and spend time sleeping or romancing with your spouse in the bedroom.

Every room serves a function or two. That which is not in keeping with those functions is most likely clutter or misplaced. Ensure that your plans take comfort and livability into account while doing this.

Decide Where to Start

Most people often are tempted to begin their decluttering and organization from cabinets and drawers underneath the sink and in the hallway. While this is okay, it is even more effective and efficient to start with areas that are visible. Begin with a small task. Select the least used and least cluttered room first. Decluttering is traumatic because it means letting go. When you start with the least cluttered room, it will reduce the traumatic nature of your task.   It's less threatening. When you conducted "Clutter Patrol" in the first preliminary exercise, you cleared out and returned your things to their rightful places. For instance, you identified all the things on the countertops, desktops, and tables that are not necessary or are not supposed to be located here and put them in the right rooms. However, you may have sadly discovered that there was "leftover stuff" for which there was no room. There were also larger objects that now occupy precious floor space. Those uncomfortable items will be relegated to the later stages of your plan. Now you can now move on to shelves, countertops, drawers, closets, and cabinets. Begin from the door and work clockwise throughout the room. Techniques for decluttering will be discussed next. Always ensure that you pay a close attention to one room at a time.

It is usually good to start with the least used room first, then move on to the next room that's used less often, and so on. The "Konmari" approach (Chapter 4) is somewhat different sequentially. Whichever method you choose depends on your personality and cleaning style.

Chapter 4:

Adopt a Technique

The Four-Box Technique

Find four boxes and a large magic marker. Bring them into the room you chose to start with. This means that you set out four boxes. One is for trash; the second is dedicated to selling, the next for donations and the last one is for stuff you plan on keeping. Label each box accordingly. Focus on visual items that are, those that are on the tops of tables and open shelves. Separate your things accordingly. Next, take your four boxes to the next room. You might find that you have already filled one of them, so you may need to start a new box to replace it.

As you put in one item after the other, ask yourself the following questions:

1. Is this object in good condition?

    If you have items in the house that are broken or tattered, then you need to throw them away. At this point, while decluttering, you do not need to dedicate things to fix if they're not important. If it is something that you want to fix, ensure that you put a timeline on when you will fix it and do it. If you're never going to get around to fixing it, toss it away.

2. If this item was broken, would I rebuy it?

    Most people have been victims of purchasing things they seldom or never use. Although you have already spent money on them, you may not need for them. Those are things you might resell or simply toss out.

3. Do I have one of these already?

    How many hair dryers do you need? How many tables do you need in the sitting area? All these questions and more are the things you need to take into consideration before decluttering seriously. You might think it's easy to get rid of all these duplicated items. It's not! Only some of items that aren't in bad condition may be sold at a garage sale. You can make some extra money on those, and you have a box for that. Other items have no resale value and deserve to be thrown out or donated.

4. Is this item worth saving?

   There are many, many things that may look attractive or useful. That ratchet set is in an attractive case, and none are missing. However, if you bought it for a temporary usage, why save it? It might now sell well. Besides, do you have sufficient closet or shelf space for it? Probably not.

5. Have I used this item for the last six months?

   If you have gone for six months without using something, then there is a high probability that you won't ever need it! That is for resale or disposal. So toss it into the appropriate box.

6. Are these "just in case" items?

When you are working on the first two rooms, you will discover a truth about your sense of security. As you categorize items, you may catch yourself thinking that you need to keep certain items "just in case" you need it for _____ someday. You may also note that these objects are usually inconsequential and inexpensive to buy. Rethink the issue and categorize accordingly.

7. Do these things fit into my future vision of life?

This is the most important question of them all. It is true that people often talk themselves into many things and even weasel their way around that question many times. However, it is you who needs to make a decision, keeping in mind your firm commitment to declutter. You have to weigh whether your choice is wise enough and in line with the vision you have for your family and home.

The truth of the matter is that no single reason can justify keeping clutter in the house. Therefore, if what you have are junky things, unnecessary duplicates, tattered or even broken items, decide to get rid of them either by selling them, donating them or discarding them.

Turn your house into a home! Ensure that the things you keep in your home are not only safe for you but also safe for your family, your guests, and your pets. People should feel comfortable and at ease whenever they are in your home. Keep your focus on your family and friends, rather than on material possessions that don't matter at all. Even your pets will demonstrate their comfort. Having friendlier surroundings has a tranquil effect on animals.

Be happy, healthy, safe and free. Do not allow stuff to control you. The only way to attain this is by living a clutter-free life forever.

The Time Segment Technique

During your house tour, you took note of the most cluttered room. Designate a time of about five minutes to a half-an-hour. Make up a "to-do list" for decluttering that room. There are some rooms that may require movement from section to section. It might be your office area or den. There are piles there, despite the fact that this is a digital world.

If you work mostly online, you are acutely aware of the junk files you've managed to create. Take that thirty minute time and clean up one folder after another. As each folder is finished, rename it, so you will recall which ones have been completed, and which ones still need attention. *Reboot your computer after you've completed each time segment. That will help you avoid computer slowdowns and frozen screens. Haven't you had the experience of hearing an apology from a clerk you've contacted to the effect that their computers are "slow today?" That's because they failed to clean up and reboot.

The Trash Bag Approach

This is a two-bag approach.

1. The Disposables

   As you rummage through your most cluttered room (including drawers and closets), you will come upon items that definitely should be disposed of. Rather than piling up twenty bags of garbage, and trudging the load out to the end of your driveway on trash day, you can decide on placing one or two additional bags out in addition to your regular disposables. This, of course, is longer-term but will save the money of having to hire a junk service. Those can become very expensive.

2. The Giveaway's

   Research online and locate charity groups that will pick up items from you. Don't worry about whether or not it is a "legitimate" charity. Someone who needs your stuff will benefit.

3. The "Turnaround"

Because you have designated your disposables and giveaway items, you have changed your attitude. It is barely noticeable when it occurs, but stands out after you've disposed of or gave away some of your stuff. You have learned how to let go of some material objects. What's more, you have noticed that your house now seems cleaner and neater. It was an enjoyable feeling, wasn't it? Try it again!

<u>Return to the rooms in your house.</u> Search inside your drawers. Ask yourself yet again why you decided to keep each of those items. You will quickly realize that parting with the other items make you feel better about yourself. It also strengthened your decision-making abilities. There are psychological rewards for this freeing behavior.

Again, decide whether or not each of the things in your drawers and closets is useful. Decide which ones bring you a sense of joy and are respected. Organize them neatly. Regarding clothing, ask yourself which ones deserve to hang up and which ones should be stored in drawers. Use the "roll-up" method of storing articles of clothing. Roll them up and stand them up vertically. Do not hesitate to leave space. Compliment yourself for having such a luxury.

The 12-12-12 Challenge

Make this challenge a part of your routine. This means that each day, you ensure that you locate 12 items to throw away, 12 to give up to charity and 12 to be taken back to their rightful position or into the rooms in your house. This challenge can be an enjoyable and exciting way to organize 36 items within a short duration. *Be sure to throw away, give away, or neatly store the items you have separated. *Do it fast before you change your mind!*

Repeat this process until there are empty areas in your drawers and on the tops of furniture.

The exercise of purging is uplifting. What's more, it will make it easier to clean and polish.

Exercise for Closet and Drawer Decluttering:

Start out by hanging all your clothes and jewelry in the reverse direction. Once you have worn them, put them back into the closets and drawers in the right direction. Once 4-6 months elapse, if you have not used some things at all, those are the items you need to discard or sell at a garage sale. Don't save clothes that are ill-fitting. Don't save clothes that are torn with the intention that you will sew them later. "Later" never happens.

Note: *Costume jewelry is valuable.* While you seldom may have worn the pin Aunt Jessie gave you, other people may find it quite attractive. If you don't want to sell it yourself or live in an area where costume jewelry is of little interest, you can always find resellers and dealers who anxiously crave it. Regardless of the distance involved, many of them will rush to your house to buy it!

The "Konmari" Method

This method is the most drastic of all and takes a lot of courage. If you have built up enough annoyance when you make your initial house tour, you will feel bound and determined to succeed with your decluttering process... If that matches your mindset, you will want to choose this approach.

1. Start with a room that is only moderately used. (No! Definitely not the kitchen!)

2. Choose to attack a closet, a cabinet or half of the drawers in a dresser.

3. Throw everything on the floor!

4. Neatly put back items that you use constantly. Don't include items that you feel you may or may not use in the next six months.

5. Grab three boxes. Label them "Trash," "Undecided," and "Give Away." Make decisions on your items, and place them in the boxes or back in the closet or drawers.

6. Move to the next closet, cabinet or set of drawers you want to tackle and do the same until you are done.

7. Continue to the next room which you use a little more often. Do up your three boxes as before. Continue on to the next room until about half the rooms are categorized in the boxes and items of use are put away.

_____

Halfway through your house, collect the items labeled "Trash" and put them into your garbage pails. Avoid second guessing.

_____

8. Return to the room with the undecided boxes. Now it's time to decide! Be firm, and separate out that which really deserves to be trashed. Add that to your garbage pails. Pull out those things that are useful enough to give away, and move them into your "Give Away" box. If you really, really feel you need an item or two

to keep, try to limit the number of saved items. Put them away neatly.

9. Now on those first few rooms, clear off the tops of your furniture. It's

   a relief to see an empty table top, doesn't it? Take some time to rejoice in that feeling. It is good for your emotional well-being.

10. Clean the tops of the furniture and polish if appropriate. Now choose just a few items to place on top. The rest can go to charity or family and friends.

Now you are ready for the heavily used rooms. Those rooms are usually the kitchen, the mudroom, the home office and den if you have one. You will need to allocate more time to those rooms, obviously.

---

11. The Infamous Kitchen

    a. A glance at your countertop. Assess the number of appliances you have stored on top, noting that some aren't used that often. However, before you can put them in your cabinets, you will have to create room for them there. Therefore, work the kitchen from the inside out – one cabinet at a time, starting with the lower cabinets. On the floor, separate the items into "always used," "used a few times a month," and "hardly ever used," and "used once or twice the past year." In two boxes separate the "hardly ever used" from the "used once or twice." Continue with the next lower cabinet and do the same. When you've finished with those boxes, temporarily put the "hardly ever used" and the "used once or twice in the past year" into another room.

    b. Now, do you have room for those extra appliances cluttering your countertop? If so, decide as to whether or not you are going to save them. Then place the ones you want to keep in the spaces in your lower cabinets. Add the "always used" items and the "used once or twice" items.

c. Repeat the same procedure with your upper cabinets.

d. Return to the items you placed temporarily in the other room. Decide if you need them. They are the items marked "hardly ever used" and "used once or twice in the past year." Dispose of accordingly.

Note: By the time you reach this stage, you will be taking more drastic measures to get rid of unneeded items and reducing clutter.

12. The Mud Room

The mudroom is easier, despite the dirt and leaves that were dragged in from outside. Clean off the boots. Examine the jackets and coats and return them to their rightful places in the house, or throw into the laundry if needed. You will note that many items are duplicates. Perhaps some of ready for the trash. Clean the mudroom floor. That is a gratifying experience, and you will want to take the time to admire the results of your efforts.

13. The Home Office and Den

Yes, the office! That will take a while if you take a lot of work home from your job or if you have a side business. By the time you decide to declutter, you will realize that you've accumulated a lot of trinkets and containers stuffed with riff-raff. Those have little to do with your work, so start on them first. Desks should have a lot of space for your daily tasks. Some people have a lot of paper files stored in file cabinets or desk drawers. Once you go through them, you may discover that they contain many antiquated items that need to be thrown into the recycling bin. Sometimes entire files are no longer needed. Once you've cleared all that out, you may find out that you need far less space.

If you use a computer, that appropriately has a "desktop." If it's a jumble, return the misplaced folders into your documents or other specific areas you've designated. Next, go through the tedious task of straightening out your folders. Attack the moderately used folders first and trash the excesses. Then move to the moderately used folders and do the same. *Reboot your computer. Otherwise, your activity will slow your computer down to a crawl. Last to attack are your often-used and current files. You may need to create new file folders for those. By now, you'll have more room for them, if needed.

Note: Take some time to explore your hard disk file, open up your applications directory, and eliminate all those pesky extra games and the like that you aren't likely to use at all. Those are usually the ones that came with your computer when you purchased it.

For your den or that of your spouse, create a more utilitarian and fun area. Rearrange furniture to be conducive to the various functions it serves. Perhaps that might mean creating a little conversational area, or an area for watching TV and playing video games, or an area for music. Then there are areas to be designated for a dart board, a pool table or card table, for example. Different types of lighting will be needed in each of those areas. Maybe there's an extra lamp in another room of little use.

The "Drop Zone"

Every house has a "drop zone." That's a haphazardly selected area where your family puts the mail, where the children put their backpacks and leftover lunches, where you and your spouse dropped the car keys, and all sorts of junk. Designate a better area for those things. Of course, food items and backpacks don't belong in the "drop zone" at all. Encourage members of your family to cooperate in that effort. Most people would prefer to procrastinate that so that it might become an important family rule. Although it takes a little extra time and effort to execute that thankless task, it will eliminate early morning panics when someone can't find something. A cluttered "drop zone" is also the reason why some folks are late with invoices. (They get mixed up with the other clutter!) Invoices should be put in a designated area on your desk. If you have room, sometimes a card table or small tall table can serve the role of a "drop zone," rather than the kitchen table, by the way!

A word about containers

Some professionals recommend that you don't use containers in which to pack your clothes or cabinet items. Certain types might be helpful, although others might not be. Be very selective when you choose containers. There are some types of clothing hangers sold that hold a multitude of dresses or pants. They are not recommended for three reasons:

1. You will be tempted to save far

too many clothes.

2. *Your clothing will get wrinkled up because everything is being crushed together.*

3. *The weight may be too heavy and the dowel in your closet will bend.*

Avoid the temptation of stacking plastic containers one on top of the other on your closet shelf. Eventually, you will need a step stool or even and ladder to reach the ones on top!

Installing smaller shelves in your closet may be very helpful. Most of those shelves aren't designed to hold a lot of excess sweaters, shirts, etc. That will help you trim down the amount of clothing you keep.

Containers that are stored in your bed are not recommended. They are inconvenient and gather dust bunnies!

Chapter 5:

Zen and the Art of Decluttering

I f you walk through your cluttered house, it rattles the mind and creates stress. All of the clutter beckons out to you and creates busy thoughts in your mind like "Oh, I should finish this...I should put that away..." What's more, the multitude of colors that these objects have subtly creates chaos in your mind. If you're used to a cluttered house, the bombardment of your senses still has a very sneaky but insidious effect.

The Purpose and Function of Zen

Zen is a mental discipline that helps one focus on just one thing. In doing so, the mind is freed up from the business of things. Healing and tranquility take place. A quiet environment creates the mood for such an experience. A non-cluttered house silently creates an atmosphere that promotes feelings of peace and self-satisfaction. Quiet and restful surroundings make it so much easier to handle an onslaught of sudden noise. That, of course, occurs when your children or your spouse burst into the door after their day's work. It works for you, too, when you get home from your work. Imagine yourself coming home from your job and collapsing into an easy chair. Think about the relief you will feel escaping the constant tapping of keys at computer keyboards, the rustling created as co-workers wander the office floor and the sporadic, excited conversations. Sit for a while and listen to the quiet.

Look at an image of a Zen garden on the Internet. It just consists of a rock or two and parallels curved lines in the sand. Why is it so alluring? Take a look at a scenic picture of sands in the desert. Likewise, there is nothing there except the sun and the gentle rolling strokes caused by the wind sweeping over the sand. People love those photos. The quiet sensations they impart are mesmerizing.

The garden and the desert scene force you to silence the wanderings of your mind. For just a few moments, you reject those mental interruptions of thought to wonder in awe and amazement at the beauty of simplicity. Slowly, calmness replaces stress, and you begin to feel peaceful. You tap into the powers of your higher self – that precious part of you which throbs and undulates with the flow of life.

Mindfulness and the Zen Technique

Dr. Jon Kabat-Zinn went to the East to learn Zen meditation to control his chronic pain. He underwent all the stages of learning the Zen technique. It worked for him, so he introduced a Westernized version of it called Mindfulness Meditation. His techniques were thoroughly researched by clinicians and results were extremely successful. Mindfulness techniques were later applied to many fields.

Mindfulness consists of taking some time to focus upon the "here-and-now," by focusing upon breathing or upon a beautiful scene (the night sky, for example). Mental discipline occurs by ignoring the intrusion of stray thoughts that have a devious way of pummeling the conscious mind. This practice brings about a sense of peace and tranquility.

That is why an uncluttered home is important. It leaves space for you to focus mentally without being distracted by clutter. Your stuff won't be strewn about, beckoning to you to engage in non-related activities. You are stable and rooted in who you are as a person, rather than what you have to do.

The Art of Decluttering and Its Beneficial Effects upon the Brain

No doubt, you've heard the terms "left-brained" and "right-brained." The "left brain" is associated with conscious thoughts and logic. The "right brain" is associated with creativity and abstract thinking. Although those two parts of your brain don't function separately from each other, the analogy holds true. A certain area of your brain (the neocortex) handles more concrete concepts like logical problem-solving, daily tasks, and the discrete interpretations of events and experiences. It is a very busy area and requires processing information. Other areas called the "right brain" handle tasks like developing new ideas, creating new and unique solutions for old and recent dilemmas, and creative expressions of yourself that release pent-up energy and communicate to others without reliance upon voice.

The combination of your logical, concrete mind of thought and your creative, ingenious mind can yield many rewards. Have you ever wondered how people developed innovative ideas and applied those creative ideas to the logic of the computer world? Those folks produce popular games, graphics programs that produce 3-D art out of a 2-D screen, new functional software, and the like. Likewise, art and music combine thought, structure and creativity.

Creativity combined with hands-on knowledge gave rise to Microsoft and Apple. True entrepreneurs rise to the top. They all thrive in uncluttered environments.

Conclusion

In this book, you have uncovered the truth and the psychological implications of consumerism. Because you felt shackled by too many products, you realized that you were looking for self-esteem and a fulfillment of your human needs in material things. After you discovered that no amount of material goods would help you become the person you wanted to be, you decided to divest yourself of your STUFF and CLUTTER. As you labored through the jungles of the paraphernalia that cluttered your house using your preferred tactical method of assault, you came to find what is most valuable to you without all the useless trappings.

Your house then became a home – a welcoming haven for you, your family and your friends. The atmosphere of your home has come to reflect you. You are unique and now live in an environment that radiates peace.

Thank you and good luck!

DECLUTTER YOUR MIND

〜〜〜〜〜 ❧❧❧❧ 〜〜〜〜〜

THE ULTIMATE GUIDE TO HAPPINESS

Chloe S

Contents

Introduction

I want to thank you and congratulate you for purchasing the book, *"DECLUTTER YOUR MIND: THE ULTIMATE GUIDE TO HAPPINESS"*

This book contains proven steps and strategies on how to achieve happiness especially to those people live the unhappy life and struggle in their life with too much messy stuff surrounding them and they are ready to change their lives completely by following this guide.

This simple guide offers the solution to happiness and the action plan to motivate your inner mind to forgive, forget and let go the past.

Many guides are going to offer advice and suggestions on what you can do declutter your mind, fix your immediate pain and overcome stress, but many of them are not true, offer bad advice, and are just too hard to follow for the long term. In this book, you will learn several ways to declutter your mind in a step by step manner, and my advice to you is that you read through it and act immediately I am sure it will help transform your life completely.

Thanks again for purchasing this book, I hope you enjoy it!

Copyright 2018 by Chloe S - All rights reserved.

or abuse of any policies, processes, or directions contained within is the solitary and utter responsibility of the recipient reader. Under no circumstances will any legal responsibility or blame be held against the publisher for any reparation, damages, or monetary loss due to the information herein, either directly or indirectly.

Respective authors own all copyrights not held by the publisher.

The information herein is offered for informational purposes solely, and is universal as so. The presentation of the information is without contract or any type of guarantee assurance.

The trademarks that are used are without any consent, and the publication of the trademark is without permission or backing by the trademark owner. All trademarks and brands within this book are for clarifying purposes only and are the owned by the owners themselves, not affiliated with this document.

Chapter 1:

What Is Stress?

What's so stressful about a few chocolate chip cookies? Nothing, if you eat two chocolate chip cookies every day as part of a well-balanced diet. Plenty, if you deprive yourself of desserts for a month, then eat an entire bag of double fudge chocolate chunk. You aren't used to all those cookies. Your body isn't used to all that sugar. That's stressful. Not stressful like totaling your car or getting transferred to Siberia, but stressful nonetheless.

According to the American Institute of Stress in Yonkers, New York, 43 percent of all adults suffer adverse health effects due to stress, and 75 percent to 90 percent of all visits to primary care physicians are for stress-related complaints or disorders.

In the same way, anything out of the ordinary that happens to you is stressful on your body. Some of that stress feels good. Even great. Without any stress at all, life would be a big bore.

Stress isn't, by definition, something bad, but it certainly isn't always good, either. In fact, it can cause dramatic health problems if it happens to you too much and for too long.

Stress isn't just out-of-the-ordinary stuff, however. Stress can also be hidden and deeply imbedded in your life. What if you can't stand your job in middle management but continue to go there every day because you're afraid of starting your own business and giving up the regular paycheck? What if your family has serious communication problems, or if you live in a place where you don't feel safe? Maybe everything seems just fine, but nevertheless you feel deeply unhappy. Even when you are accustomed to certain things in your life — dirty dishes in the sink, family members that don't help you out, twelve-hour days at the office — those things can be stressful. You might even get stressed out when something goes right. Maybe someone is nice to you and you become suspicious, or you feel uncomfortable if your house is too clean. You are so used to things being difficult that you don't know how to adjust. Stress is a strange and highly individual phenomena.

Unless you live in a cave without a television (actually, not a bad way to eliminate stress in your life), you've probably heard quite a bit about stress in the media, around the coffee machine at work, or in the magazines and newspapers you read. Most people have a preconceived notion of what stress is in general, as well as what stress is to them. What does stress mean to you?

- Discomfort?

- Pain?

- Worry?

- Anxiety?

- Excitement?

- Fear?

- Uncertainty?

These things cause people stress and are mostly conditions stemming from stress. But what is stress itself? Stress is such a broad term, and there are so many different kinds of stress affecting so many people in so many different ways that the word **stress** may seem to defy definition. What is stressful to one person might be exhilarating to another. So, what exactly is stress?

Stress comes in several guises, some more obvious than others. Some stress is acute, some is episodic, and some is chronic. Let's take a closer look at each kind of stress and how it affects you.

Stress Relief

for Your Mind

and Spirit

Stress management techniques that strengthen and reinforce the body will also help to strengthen the mind's ability to resist the negative effects of stress. But some stress management techniques directly deal with the mind — the thought processes, emotions, intellect, and, extending beyond the mind, the quest for spiritual meaning. In this chapter, we'll look at meditation techniques, which are the most effective techniques targeted to your mind and spirit.

The Negative Mental Effects of Stress

- An inability to concentrate
- Excessive, uncontrollable worrying
- Feelings of anxiety and panic
- Forgetfulness
- Sadness, depression
- Nervousness
- Fatigue, low energy
- Irritability
- Restlessness
- Negativism
- Fearfulness
- Unrealistic expectations
- Despair

Yes, some of these symptoms of stress can be directly connected to the body, but these symptoms are often a product of the mind and its interpretation of and obsession with or attachment to stressful events. How do you stress-proof your mind? With mental stress management, of course.

Stress management for the mind and the spirit is specifically targeted to help still, calm, and quiet the overactive mind, which is so common in people who are experiencing stress beyond their stress tolerance levels. These techniques help you to recognize the thought processes that are increasing your stress, the attitudes that can trigger a stress response, and the way you tend to cling to ideas as if they were life preservers. They can also fulfill the desire for higher meaning that, when thwarted by a life that isn't what we wanted it to be, can slowly erode our happiness and self-esteem.

Some of these techniques are related to physical stress management techniques (specifically, relaxation techniques) because, again, mind and body are inextricably connected. But if you are experiencing even a few of the mental negative effects of stress or feel that your spirit is sorely in need of reinforcements and want to go straight to the source, try these stress management techniques for mind and spirit.

Stress on Your Body

You can control some of the stresses on your body; for example, you can determine how much you eat and how much you exercise. These stresses fall into the physiological stressor category. Then, there are environmental stressors, such as environmental pollution and substance addiction.

1. **Environmental stressors.** These are things in your immediate environment that put stress on your physical body. These include air pollution, polluted drinking water, noise pollution, artificial lighting, bad ventilation, or the presence of allergens in the field of ragweed outside your bedroom window or in the dander of the cat who likes to sleep on your pillow.

2. **Physiological stressors.** These are the stressors within your own body that cause stress. Bad health habits such as smoking, drinking too much, eating junk food, or being sedentary put physiological stress on your body. So does illness, whether it's the common cold or something more serious like heart disease or cancer. Injury also puts stress on your body — a

broken leg, a sprained wrist, and a slipped disk are all stressful.

One of the most common reactions to stress is compulsive eating. The best way to handle your temporary weakness is to find a healthier way to deal with your stressful feelings. A large glass of water, a walk around the block, or a phone call to a friend might be just what you need. Just remember, you can control your life.

Just as potent but less direct are stressors that impact your body by way of your mind. For example, getting caught in heavy traffic may stress your body directly because of the air pollution it creates, but it may also stress your body indirectly because you get so worked up and irritated sitting in your car in the middle of a traffic jam that your blood pressure rises, your muscles tense, and your heart beats faster. If you were to interpret the traffic jam differently — say, as an opportunity to relax and listen to your favorite CD before getting to work — your body might not experience any stress at all. Again, attitude plays a major role.

Pain is another, trickier example of indirect stress. If you have a terrible headache, your body may not experience direct physiological stress, but your emotional reaction to the pain might cause your body significant stress. People tend to be fearful of pain, but pain is an important way to let us know something is wrong. Pain can signal injury or disease. However, sometimes we already know what's wrong. We get migraines, or have arthritis, or experience menstrual cramps, or a bad knee acts up when the weather changes. This kind of "familiar" pain isn't useful in terms of alerting us to something that needs immediate medical attention.

But because we know we are in some form of pain, we still tend to get tense. "Oh no, not another migraine! No, not today!" Our emotional reaction doesn't cause the pain, but it does cause the physiological stress associated with the pain. Pain in itself isn't stressful. Our reaction to pain is what causes stress. So, learning stress management techniques may not stop pain, but it can stop the physiological stress associated with pain.

Therapies designed to help people manage chronic pain counsel patients to explore the difference between pain and the negative interpretation of pain. People living with chronic pain learn meditation techniques for entering and confronting pain apart from the brain's interpretation of the pain as a source of suffering.

When your body is experiencing this stress response, whether caused by direct or indirect physiological stressors, it undergoes some very specific changes. Around the beginning of the twentieth century, physiologist Walter B. Cannon coined the phrase "fight or flight" to describe the biochemical changes stress invokes in the body, preparing it to flee or confront danger more safely and effectively. These are the changes that happen in your body every time you feel stressed, even if running away or fighting aren't relevant or wouldn't help you (for example, if you're about to give a speech, take a test, or confront your mother-in-law about her constant unsolicited advice, neither fight nor flight are very helpful responses).

Here's what happens inside your body when you feel stress:

1. Your cerebral cortex sends an alarm message to your hypothalamus, the part of your brain that releases the chemicals that create the stress

response. Anything your brain **perceives** as stress will cause this effect, whether or not you are in any real danger.

2. Your hypothalamus releases chemicals that stimulate your sympathetic nervous system to prepare for danger.

3. Your nervous system reacts by raising your heart rate, respiration rate, and blood pressure. Everything gets turned "up."

4. Your muscles tense, preparing for action. Blood moves away from the extremities and your digestive system, into your muscles and brain. Blood sugars are mobilized to travel to where they will be needed most.

5. Your senses get sharper. You can hear better, see better, smell better, taste better. Even your sense of touch becomes more sensitive.

Chapter 2:

What is Clutter?

Realize that you can vanquish anything and get anything you need. Why is it hard for some? All things considered, this is a direct result of mental mess.

Mental perplexity is only musings, emotions, and tension that is bunched up in your mind and leads you into a condition of self-disrupt, enduring, battle, stress, and partition. Mental mess makes life hard and confused. The stuff puts us inconsistent with every other person. We can't see it, yet mental perplexity sneaks where peace and love don't. In the event that we are jumbled, we are opposing the regular stream and simplicity of life. We are not enabling ourselves to achieve our maximum capacity or finding our genuine's implications.

Like I said earlier in the event that you hold a serious conviction of what you have is as of now there, at that point you will show it in your life. When you have mental mess, it gets muddled;

you will have excessively numerous considerations driving your psyche to head in a wide range of bearings. Possibly there is a voice inside your head saying that it is all good for nothing. At that point you have another voice in your mind saying that it is everything to you and that you ought to never surrender. Also, at last the inquiry comes to which one to take after? Furthermore, noting this will be hard.

On the off chance that you are not encountering transparency, peace, and adore, you have mental mess. It lives solely in your musings. What's more, it just takes one negative idea or feeling to misdirect you into a substantially more critical and ruinous life. Presently, there are eight standard indications of mental mess.

Chapter 3:

Causes of Mental Clutter

Mental clutter is caused by a variety of factors. Before you learn about these factors, it is **crucial** to determine about psychological confusion first.

In the story, there was a man who wanted to hang a painting on the wall. He had a nail, but he did not have a hammer. So, he thought of going to his neighbor's house to borrow a stick. However, he started to have **doubts**.

What if his neighbor **refused** to lend him his hammer? His neighbor barely spoke to him the day before. Perhaps, he was in a hurry. Maybe he had something against him. Why would he hold anything against him when he did not do anything wrong?

If his neighbor wanted to borrow something, he would readily lend it. So, why would he refuse to let him borrow a hammer? These types of people are the ones that make others miserable, he thought. Even worse, he might **feel** that he needed him because of the hammer.

With such thoughts, the man rushed to his neighbor's house and yelled mean things at him before his neighbor even had any idea of why he came to his door.

This story illustrates what a mentally cluttered person is like. Clutter is the junk that floats around in a mentally cluttered person's head. It is what causes him to jump to ridiculous and unreasonable conclusions.

Mental Clutter

Mental clutter is the trash that you hoard in your mind. It can cause you to think of the worst. It can keep you pessimistic, fearful, and anxious, trapped in the web of your making. It can also save you **stuck** in self-sabotage, struggle, suffering, separation, and stress. It can make your life complicated and confusing. It can even put you at odds with everyone else.

Mental clutter is hidden from the naked eye. It also lurks in places where there is no love or peace. The longer you stay cluttered, the longer you resist the ease and flow of life.

If you do not experience peace, love, and clarity, your mind is cluttered. The mental clutter is elusive and exclusive in your thoughts. It begins as a head for, which is misleading and cloudy. Slowly but surely, it evolves into something **bigger** and **worse**.

Your mental clutter consists of stories that you tell yourself. These are the stories that cripple your potential and attack your wellbeing. It says you that you cannot, should not, and will not. It gives you a reason to distrust and doubt, leaving you feeling helpless. It tells you of lies of lack and limitation **instead** of the truth regarding wealth and abundance.

When it accumulates and blinds you to the truth of who you are, without any limiting beliefs, you become the man who was in need of a hammer and who spiraled down the rabbit hole. You become a person who believes that he is not good enough, does not deserve to be loved, and will not have what he wants. When you clear away this mess, the truth is revealed.

Chapter 4:

Symptoms of Clutter

How can you tell if you already have too much clutter? There are eight telltale symptoms that you have to watch out for. When you notice these symptoms starting to show, you need to start decluttering.

Confusion

This refers to the **lack** of understanding and clarity. It is uncertainty or being unclear about certain things. When you are confused, you feel scattered and out of sorts. It causes you to start being fearful and worried.

Chatter

This refers to the ongoing narrative at the back of your head. It is jibber jabber, noise, and inner dialogue. It feels like a constant mental dialogue that drones on in your background. It is impatient and curious.

Chaos

This refers to the total disarray, disorder, disruption, and disorganization in your head. It leads to **mental anarchy** and feels like having no organization or order in spite of dissenting beliefs and ideas.

Conditions

These are defined as stipulations, prerequisites, or requirements. They also refer to factors that influence outcomes or progressions of certain situations. They are the expectations and demands that people place on themselves and others. They can seem like boundaries, limits, and rules.

Collections

These refer to the grouping or gathering of objects. They see to the stockpiling of security, comfort, and prestige. They can feel like validation and trophies of acknowledgment.

Comparisons

These refer to the formation of superlative or comparative judgments. Comparison **deliberately** takes two things and pits them against each other to select a preference or winner. It can feel like searching for something better and more prominent.

Commitments

These refer to the allocation of energy to different activities or causes within a particular timeframe. You commit to both **action** and **attention** to everything, including work, family, health, and hobbies. Commitments can feel like filling your calendar with obligations and appointments.

Control

This refers to the power to influence behaviors or courses of events. Through it, you can seek to enslave the action and performance of your life so that you can get your desired results. It can feel like manipulating and managing circumstances to make you more comfortable.

Chapter 5:

Clutter and its Impact on Life

People collect things for different reasons. Some people think they will need to use those words later on or perhaps their future children would use them. Others collect items because they have an **emotional attachment** to them. After all, a lot of people like to keep things that have sentimental value. There are also those who feel like they would only be **wasting** money if they throw away their expensive things, no matter how old, broken, or useless they are already.

You may be holding on to a nice pair of shoes you have not worn in years because you **believe** there will come an occasion where you can wear them again. You may keep refusing to donate unread books that take up a **lot** of space in your room because you keep telling yourself there will come a time when you will finally read them. There are indeed lots of reasons why people hold onto their things.

The truth, however, is that you **probably** just made a mistake purchasing or acquiring those things in the first place. This can be **difficult** for your brain to process. Researchers at Yale University said that there are two areas of your mind that are linked to pain. These are the insula and the anterior cingulate cortex. They light up as a response when you let go of things that you feel connected to.

Your anterior cingulate cortex is the **same** area of your brain that lights up whenever you experience physical pain. It views the loss of clutter as something that causes physical pain. This explains why the more you financially or emotionally commit to a thing, the **stronger** your desire gets to keep it.

Every time you introduce a new item into your life, you readily associate it with value. This makes it more **difficult** for you to give it up or let it go when it is time to do so. Because of your psychological connection to things, you start to accumulate **more**.

The Effect of Clutter on the Brain

There is a misconception that hoarding things is **not** harming anyone. It hurts the hoarder. Hoarding is a severe obsessive-compulsive disorder that requires a **long-term solution**. It does not only affect the patient, but it also affects the people living with him as well as those who care about his wellbeing.

Having unnecessary things around can hurt your ability to process information and retain your focus. Your attachment to clutter can result in stress, depression, and embarrassment. It can also endanger your life if your hoarding goes out of control.

For example, if you fill your house with junk, you may no longer be able to **move** around, and you may be in **danger** of things falling on you. You may also have a hard time maintaining proper hygiene, causing you to develop infections and illnesses. Also, your house can be infested with rats and other pests because of all the garbage.

Neuroscientists at Princeton University have found that physical clutter tends to compete for attention. This causes **increased** stress and

diminished performance. You will not be able to perform appropriately in an unorganized environment because the mess and clutter around you will keep you distracted.

Researchers at the University of California, Los Angeles (UCLA) did a study that involved several mothers as participants. At the end of it, they found that the stress hormones of all the participants **spiked** when they dealt with their personal belongings. Thus, it was concluded that physical clutter overloads the senses just as multitasking overwhelms the brain. As a result, you become more stressed out, and your ability to focus and think creatively **diminishes** when clutter surrounds you.

Peter Walsh, a well-known author, and host of reality television series Extreme Clutter said that things left undone might be your **undoing**. Clutter only adds stress and wastes valuable time. Unorganized individuals with cluttered lives tend to feel anxious, out of control, and frustrated. They often have a hard time relaxing and unwinding as well.

So, if you want to have more peace of mind, you **need** to declutter and organize your belongings and surroundings. Decluttering generates fresh energy, releases negative emotions, and creates physical and mental space.

Clutter Is Not Merely Physical

Papers, carton boxes, bottles, plastic bags, broken appliances, and other material items are not the **only** clutter in your home. Even the files in your computer can be regarded as clutter. Digital clutter can be **just** as bad as physical clutter. When you have too many unnecessary files on your computer, you may be distracted. You may have a hard time focusing on work and completing tasks.

For example, if you have so many items on your to-do list, you may feel overwhelmed and get confused about what to do **first**. If you keep receiving notifications, your brain may not have a chance to process the experience entirely. In essence, if your mind has **too much** going on in it, its power decreases. This can give you a hard time filtering information, maintaining an active working memory, and quickly switch between tasks.

Chapter 6:

Declutter your mind and manage stress

What best mitigates weight is similarly person. You may have endeavored some direct sounding conditions for managing your weight and found that they aren't that helpful.

The Power of Stress Management

Stress organization tips are tied in with helping you develop a convincing weight organization system. Effective weight organization relies upon an attempted, careful approach that fuses both cognizance of stress and lifestyle changes.

The going with six clues are laid out by virtue of that.

Tip 1: Identify affinities and practices that show weight

It's definitely not hard to recognize wellsprings of stress following an imperative life event, for instance, advancing occupations, moving home, or losing a companion or relative, yet pinpointing the purposes behind common weight can be more trapped. It's extremely not by any means clear your considerations, notions, and practices that add to your sentiments of tension. Obviously, you may understand that you're for the most part worried over work due dates, yet maybe it's your postponing, rather than the certifiable movement asks for, that is causing the weight.

To recognize your correct wellsprings of stress, look at your inclinations, perspective, and reasons:

Do you clear up away criticalness as brief ("I just have a million things going on the present minute") in spite of the way that you can't recall the last time you chilled?

Do you portray stress as a fundamental bit of your work or home life ("Things are always crazy around here") or as a bit of your personality ("I have a lot of restless essentialness that is it more or less")?

Do you blame your stress for different people or outside events, or view it as inside and out normal and unexceptional?

Until the point that the moment that you recognize obligation with respect to the part you play in making or caring for it, your sentiment uneasiness will remain outside your control.

Start your weight journal

A weight journal can empower you to perceive the reliable stressors for the duration of your life and the way you oversee them. Each time you grab centered; make sure to screen it in your journal. The thing is this: as you keep a step by step log of these events, you will begin to see illustrations and normal themes with these stressors.

Thusly, record these things in your journal:

What caused your weight (figure in case you aren't sure?)

How might you feel, both physically and deep down?

How might you act on account of the stressor?

What did you move forward?

Tip 2: Replace terrible adjusting techniques to sound ones

By and by, consider the routes you starting at now administer and adjust to stress in your life. Your weight journal can empower you to remember them. Are the adjusting frameworks you apply sound or terrible, strong or ineffectual? Heartbreakingly, people have a tendency to adjust to stress in ways that compound their worry.

There are tragic ways people have a tendency to adjust to weight. These adjusting frameworks may by chance diminish weight, in any case they cause more mischief as time goes on:

Smoking

Using pills or meds to loosen up

Drinking substantially more than you should

Resting more than you should

Pigging out on so much junk or comfort support

Deferring your activities/commitments

Wandering off in fantasy land for an impressive period of time since you are looking phone

Finishing off every snapshot of the day since you are running from your issues

Pulling once more from colleagues, family, and activities and staring off into space

Taking out your weight on others out of disappointment

In case these systems you apply don't add to your more basic eager and physical prosperity, by then the open door has just traveled every which way to find more useful ones. No single approach works out for everyone neither in every situation, so certification to investigate distinctive roads with respect to various strategies and systems. Focus on what impacts you to feel calm and in charge of your case.

Tip 3: Get moving and gain ground

Unknowingly, physical activity accept a gigantic vital part in diminishing and keeping the effects of weight, yet you don't should be a contender nor put hours in a rec focus to experience the points of interest. Practically any kind of physical activity can enable straightforwardness to weight and expend with outrageous warmth all the shock, strain, and frustration. Exercise tends to release endorphins that reason a lift in your perspective and impacts you to feel phenomenally right, and it can moreover fill in as a critical preoccupation to your step by step pushes.

Regularly, most extraordinary favorable circumstances rise up out of honing for 30 minutes or more, yet you can start pretty much nothing and build up your wellbeing level consistently. Short, 10-minute impacts of activity tend to lift your heart rate and impact you to break out into a sweat which supports you relieve weight and give you greater essentialness and optimism.

Manage your stress with standard exercise

By and by, once you're in the inclination for being physically powerful, do endeavor to intertwine standard exercise into your entire step by step design. Activities that are diligent and cadenced—which require moving both your arms and your legs—are most especially practical at decreasing weight. Walking, running, swimming, moving, cycling, tai - chi, and oxygen devouring classes are extraordinary choices.

Pick that one activity you acknowledge as this makes you more slanted to remain with it. While working out, try to focus on your body and all physical (and as a less than dependable rule excited) sensations you experience as you're moving and not on your contemplations. Adding this care segment to your action routine won't simply empower you to break out of the cycle of negative contemplations that oftentimes runs with overwhelming weight, however helps move your essentialness, positive imperativeness, to the most centered around part of your body. While working out, constantly focus on sorting out your breathing with every advancement you make. For example, endeavor to perceive how the air or sunlight feels on your skin. Simply getting away from your head and concentrating on how you feel while doing these is the surest technique to refrain from getting harm and clean yourself up.

Tip 4: Connect to people

Social engagement has been believed to be the speediest and most capable way to deal with lessen and chop down a leg on push and go without going over the edge to inside or external events that are believed to incapacitate. Getting the chance to express what you're encountering can be to a great degree cathartic, paying little respect to whether it shows up there is nothing you can do to alter that particular troubling situation. We in general know the slant having a calmed slant in the wake of talking with someone else who impacts us to feel shielded and got on. This specific experience of security—as observed and related to us by our tangible framework—occurs in light of nonverbal signs that begin from what we hear, see and feel.

The internal ear, face, heart, and stomach are wired together in such a course to the mind that social relationship with another person versus through looking, listening carefully, talking, et cetera can quickly calm you down and put the brakes on protected weight responses like "fight or-flight." It furthermore releases hormones that move to diminish weight, paying little mind to whether you can't alter that particular unsavory situation itself. In all trustworthiness, it's not for the most part sensible to have a mate close by to slant toward, to talk when you feel overwhelmed by weight, yet it hints at change when you amass and keep up an arrangement of dear colleagues who will empower you to improve your flexibility to life's stressors. On the contrary side, the all the more devastate and separated you are yourself, the higher you lack of protection to weight.

Contact your family and friends and routinely relate up close and personal, and not through calls. The real thing here is that people you banter with don't need the ability to settle your weight; they basically ought to be right group of onlookers individuals to you. Opening up isn't an indication of weakness as you may think and it won't make you a weight to others. Honestly, most colleagues will be complimented that you trust them okay to confide in them about what you are experiencing, and it won't simply fortify your cooperation bond yet what's more upgrade your success. Likewise, remember, it's never past the point where it is conceivable to develop new fellowships and strengthen your empowering gathering of individuals paying little heed to whether you figure your mien towards people can never hint at change.

Tip 5: Try and put aside a couple of minutes for excitement just and loosening up

When you go past an accept accountability approach and an elevating perspective, you can reduce stress in your life by means of individual out a touch of "individual" time. Make an effort not to get so compensated for lost time in the humming about of your life that you disregard to manage your own specific needs. Supporting yourself is a need you have to educate into your life, not an indulgence. If you frequently put aside a couple of minutes for excitement and loosening up, you will easily have the ability to manage life's stressors as you have a better limit successfully than loosen up when you feel centered.

Set aside a particular time to loosen up. Fuse "Bona fide" rest in your step by step design.

"Authentic" here induces not loosening up with clearing bills what not. Do whatever it takes not to empower distinctive duties regarding assault starting at now.

Chapter 7:

How to Reframe Negative Thoughts

Negative thoughts can **drag you down** and leave you paralyzed with anxiety or depression. They make you feel demotivated and discouraged. They make you walk around with a rain cloud over your head all the time. If you continue to harbor negative thoughts, you will hold yourself back and prevent yourself from living life the way you **want** to.

The best way to overcome your negative thoughts is make an effort to change the way you think. When you change your mindset, you will be able to change your behavior. The following tips are effective in helping people overcome their negative thoughts and replace them with more positive ones: Find what is helpful or good when you find yourself in a seemingly negative situation.

Everybody, including the most successful people in the world, experiences setbacks and failures. When you do not get what you want, you may feel negative emotions and cause you to see things in a negative manner. When this happens, you have to **counter** it by asking certain questions. These questions should help you feel better as well as help you grow.

For example, you can ask yourself what good thing you can see in the situation or what you can do differently in case you find yourself in the same situation in the future. You can **also** ask yourself about the lesson that you have learned from the experience. Furthermore, you can put yourself in the shoes of other people. What do you think your friends will tell you or advise you to do to effectively deal with the situation you are in.

Remind yourself that other people do not really care about what you do or say.

You may end up with negative thoughts when you start thinking that other people may think or say **something** about you. This causes you to over analyze things to the point of no longer being rational. If you continue to do this, you will soon lose touch of reality and get caught up in your negative thoughts.

You have to realize that people do not really have a lot of energy or time to talk about you or think about the things you do. In fact, they are too consumed with their own lives, which include issues with their jobs, children, finances, *etc*. They have their **own** worries and fears, so they will not think twice about yours.

If you remind yourself of this truth, you will be set free from constraints. You will be able to take the necessary steps to reach your own goals and live your life the way you have always wanted to.

Question your thoughts.

Every time you catch yourself having negative thoughts, you should start questioning them. Ask yourself if you have to take the negative thought seriously or play with it. The answer is most likely a 'no'. You can lighten up your situation by playing or challenging your negative thoughts to lessen their impact.

You also have to analyze the situation. Find out why you came up with negative thoughts in the first place. The root cases can vary. You may be hungry, tired, or even bored. Whatever the reason is, you have to deal with it **accordingly**.

When you question your negative thoughts, you make yourself grounded. You become levelheaded and you gain a more **sensible** perspective. You realize that experiencing negativity does not erase the fact that positivity **still** exists.

Replace negativity with positivity.

Look around you. What do you see? What do you allow inside your mind? Whatever your answer is, it has a **huge** effect on your life. Thus, you have to be mindful of the thoughts that you allow inside your mind.

Question yourself regarding the top three negativity sources you have. The answer may pertain to people, music, social media, *etc*. Then, you have to question yourself about what you can do to **lessen** the amount of time you spend on these negativity sources.

Make it a point to follow up on this. Spend less time on your negativity sources and more time on your positivity sources. It is always a **better** idea to go with the positive.

Refrain from turning molehills into mountains.

To **prevent** negative thoughts from growing inside your mind, you have to confront them as soon as possible. Do not allow negative things to get worse. You can zoom out of them by asking yourself if your current problems are still going to matter several weeks, months, or years from now. You will realize that they are really just nothing. Refrain from turning such molehills of negativity into mountains of negativity.

Release your negative thoughts and talk about them.

Sometimes, letting things out and talking them over is the best solution to a problem. If you keep your negative thoughts inside your mind, they will grow. Hence, you have to release them. You can talk to a friend or a therapist. **Venting** about the issues you have within you can help you unload the burden that you feel. It can also help you change your perspective about your situation and encourage you to search for **feasible** solutions or courses of action.

Live your life and then come back to the moment.

If you find yourself starting to harbor negative thoughts, you might be recalling a past event or anticipating a future one. Your moods can be confusing and your thoughts troubling.

To get rid of such thoughts, you have to fully focus on the present moment. Be mindful of whatever is happening to your right at that moment. When you focus on the present, you will be more open-minded and less likely to engage in negative thinking.

One way to encourage yourself to focus on your present moment is to focus on your breathing. Pause for a minute or two and then take deep breaths. When you inhale, the air should go in through your nose and fill up your belly. Then, it should go out through your mouth. As you **repeatedly** inhale and exhale, you have to focus on the air going in and out of your body alone. Do not think of anything else during this time.

Another ideal way how you can focus on your present moment is to observe your surroundings and focus on the things that you see. **Take a break** for one to two minutes, get your thoughts out of your mind, and then concentrate on the things that you see around you. You can also focus on the passers-by, the birds, the trees, the clouds, the warmth of the sun on your skin, the smell of the freshly baked bread, or even the traffic noise in the streets.

Go to the gym for a quick workout session.

Exercise gives you endorphins, which are natural chemicals that can make you **happier**. Each time you feel down, you should exercise. If you have a hectic schedule and you cannot afford half an hour for a workout, you can simply do ten to fifteen minutes.

The important thing is that you did it. It does not matter how long you exercised, as long as you did it. In addition, working out helps you distract yourself from your negative thoughts. It helps you attain focus and may even **encourage** you to harbor positive thoughts.

Do not allow your negative thoughts to bring you down.

A lot of people make the **mistake** of letting their fears get the best of them. If you are one of these people, you may choose to run away from your issues instead of facing them. You may have the impulse to avoid your fears, but you have to **understand** that they can get worse if you do not deal with them properly.

One way to deal with a situation like this is to ask yourself about the worst possible case that can happen. Eventually, you will realize that the worst-case scenario is not that bad. You will also be prompted to take action and reduce the possibility of it actually occurring. When you do this, you will have **clarity** and your fear will be **lessened**.

Aim to help other people achieve positivity in their lives.

If you allow yourself to be stuck with your negative thinking patterns, you will not improve and grow as a person. Thus, you have to get out of your head. Do not let yourself have a victim mindset. Redirect your energy onto positivity. Aim to help others. When you do this, you will feel better as well as become more optimistic. You can **help** another person gain positivity in their life by being kind, listening to them, and saying good things about them. It is important to be genuine.

Practice gratitude and be thankful for everything that you have.

When you become grateful for the little things that you have, you become more **appreciative** of the bigger things that you receive. You also open yourself up for more blessings. Oftentimes, people get so caught up in their day to day lives that they forget to appreciate the wonderful things they have around them.

Each morning, make an **effort** to notice the blessings that you have such as sunlight, water, food, air, *etc.* You tend to neglect these things because you are used to having them on a daily basis. Imagine your life without them and you would be surprised of how much you actually need them. When you become grateful for your blessings, you receive more good things.

Neuro-Linguistic Programming

Neuro-Linguistic Programming (NLP) involves neurology, language, and programming – the three most **influential** components that produce human experience. It is an epistemology or a pragmatic school of thought that addresses issues associated with human nature.

It focuses on two presuppositions: life and mind are systematic processes, which means that your body, the universe, and societies all form complex systems and subsystems that mutually influence and interact with one another; and the map is not the territory, which means that you can have your own perception of reality but cannot really know it because you are only human.

NLP offers ways on how you can **alter** your thinking patterns. It can help you change how you think, approach your life, and view events from your past. It is efficient and practical. It can help you control your mind and your life in general. However, unlike psychoanalysis, it does not focus on 'why' but rather on 'how'.

The main principle behind NLP is that even though you cannot control **every** aspect of your life, you can still control the way you think and act towards various situations. Certain external factors are out of your control, such as accidents, death, and failed relationships. It is up to you how you will perceive them. It is really what goes on **in** your head that matters.

Keep in mind that your feelings and thoughts are neither things that you *have* nor *are*, but rather what you *do*. Usually, their causes are complicated and may even involve beliefs or comments from other people. Through NLP, you can learn how to take control of these influences and beliefs. You can learn how to get over your **greatest** fears and phobias as well.

The following methods should be done in order to decrease mental clutter:

Disassociation

Emotions can **greatly** affect actions. You can get angry, upset, or stressed out in an instant, causing you to do things without thinking them through. For example, when somebody upsets you, you may respond by saying hurtful words or getting revenge.

With NLP, you can learn how to neutralize your negative emotions by viewing situations in an objective manner. This allows you to be **more reasonable**.

To practice the technique of disassociation, you have to identify the emotion that you want to eliminate. This can be fear, uneasiness, or dislike of a certain person, object, event, or location.

Visualize yourself being in this situation from the **very** beginning. However, instead of viewing yourself as the main participant, you should view yourself as a mere observer.

Play the scenario backwards and then fast forward and backwards again in your head, as if you are watching a movie on the big screen. You can add music for a more dramatic effect. Choose something funny and light so that you will **also** feel lighter. Repeat this step three to four times more.

Next, visualize the event as something that occurs in the present. Notice your emotions towards the stimuli changing or disappearing. If you still have the same negative emotions as you did before, you should keep doing this exercise until your negative emotions completely vanish.

Content Reframing

Whenever you find yourself stuck in a situation in which you feel angry or powerless, you can try content reframing. It can help you change how you perceive your current situation, so you can view it in a different frame or more empowering way.

To help you understand content reframing better, consider this scenario: You have just been let go from work. You have no job. If you think about it, a lot of things can go wrong from this situation. You have no more source of income, so you will **eventually** drain your bank account. When you use up all your savings, you will not be able to pay rent, buy food, and commute. You will become homeless, be at risk of illnesses, or even starve to death.

Then again, you can also view the same situation in a different context. How can you do this? Rather than go with the negative outcome, you should go with the positive possibility.

Since you no longer have this job, you now have more time to focus on what you want as well as explore different areas of expertise. You can develop more skills and hone your talents. It can also be a learning opportunity. Through your mistakes, you can come up with better decisions and find ways on how to improve your work.

Having this kind of adversity can also make you stronger. You have experienced rock bottom, so you should now be more motivated to get back up. Ten years from now, you can look back at this experience and feel so much better because you have come a long way.

You can **always** reframe your content. You can change the way you view situations and take your focus away from the negativity. This allows you to view the situation in a completely different manner. When you focus on the positive, it becomes **easier** to come up with better and more reasonable decisions.

Refrain from panicking and thinking fear-based thoughts because this will only cause you to have deeper problems and more failures. Remember that every situation has both good and bad points. Instead of focusing on the bad, you should focus on the good.

Self-Anchoring

In NLP, self-anchoring is used to obtain an emotional response to words said or actions done.

For example, people may smile unconsciously when you touch their shoulder. A girl may response in shock when you pull her hair. It is possible to **instantaneously** change the way you feel. When you are angry, upset, or insecure, don't worry because such negative feeling can quickly go away. You just have to anchor a positive emotional response to it and fire this anchor every time you start to feel the negative emotion.

Determine the state that you wish to experience, whether it is happiness, excitement, *etc*. Do everything you can to reach that particular state. Your body language can do wonders. Try sitting straight, smiling, or doing a power pose. You can also try recalling a happy memory.

Once you reach that state, visualize a smoke circle in front of you. Then, imagine yourself stepping inside that circle and feeling **great**. Hold this visualization until you feel positive energy flow within your body.

Now, it is time to get out of the circle. Imagine yourself stepping **outside** and thinking of something else. The purpose behind this is to have a different emotion. You should feel something else that is completely unrelated to your previous one.

After a while, imagine yourself going back **inside** the circle. Observe how you respond to this move. If you feel the same emotion as you did when you previously stepped inside the circle, then you know that the technique has worked.

Rapport

It is **important** to build rapport with others. It is vital not only for succeeding in life, but also for gaining peace of mind and getting rid of mental clutter.

You can follow the breathing patterns or mirror the body languages of other people. Try to be as natural as you can. You can also use the same words that they use. Make sure that you are **discreet**.

You can also assess their primary sensory perception, whether it is auditory or kinesthetic. Then, you can use that same perception yourself. You can pay attention to their choice of words or just talk to them.

You can tell that the primary sensory perception of a person is auditory if that person makes use of words or phrases such as "I am listening to you", "I hear you", or "She has a loud voice". It is **actually** easy to determine primary sensory perception. It is auditory if noise and sound are involved.

On the **other** hand, you can tell that the primary sensory perception of a person is visual if he uses words or phrases such as "You have a bright future", "My vision is very clear", or "I see what you mean". In essence, the primary sensory perception is visual if it involves darkness, brightness, glitter, or any other elements that can be seen.

A person has a **kinesthetic** primary sensory perception if he uses words or phrases such as "He has a pleasant vibe", "I do not feel right about this" or "I have a good feeling about this". The primary sensory perception is kinesthetic if it involves touch, warmth, coolness, or any other element that can be felt.

Changing Beliefs

Whatever you believe in will **eventually** come true. This is what the Law of Attraction, one of the Universal laws, states. Whatever you **constantly** think about and whatever you believe with all your heart can eventually happen.

If you have positive beliefs, then you can see a bright future ahead of you. On the contrary, if you keep harboring negative and limiting beliefs, you can always experience mishaps and other misfortunate events.

There are three fundamental types of limiting beliefs, and these are: beliefs about meaning, beliefs about cause, and beliefs about identity. Each of these beliefs can influence the way you perceive the world. They can also affect the way you filter out parts of reality that do not fit with your belief **system**. It is **actually** your beliefs that let you experience awareness with regard to the different aspects of reality that harmonize with them.

Your beliefs are powerful since they can determine the experiences that you will have in your life. They are **developed** when you encounter something that relates to your experiences. For example, you may experience something bad or damaging. It is up to you how you will handle it.

You can either let it consume your entire being or learn from it and move on with your life. Whichever option you choose, it will most likely attract the same experiences. These experiences will, then, **reaffirm** the rightness you have about these situations.

If it is possible to go straight to content reframing, then you will no longer form such beliefs in the first place. Sadly, many people have a tendency to dwell on the negative experience. This causes them to have similar negative experiences. The worse thing is that they do not realize the connection, and they become surprised when they continue to **experience** negativity in their lives.

It is important to realize that situations are **neither** bad nor good. It is only the way you view them that makes them bad or good. If you choose to view them as a negative thing, then you will form a negative or **limiting** belief that causes you to have the same experiences that affirm such negative belief. If you continue to do this, your negative beliefs will deepen and worsen over time.

If you focus on the negative, you filter out your experiences, causing you to repeat your negative beliefs. For example, you have just gotten out of an abusive relationship. Your former partner cheated and treated you badly. Obviously, this experience has had a huge effect on you.

Then again, would you learn from it and do your best to avoid making the same mistakes or would you start to believe that all men are liars, cheaters, and bad people? If you choose the latter, then you have **already** formed a limiting belief, which is not healthy for you.

To change limiting beliefs, you should acquire more data about situations. Do not disregard the positive facts by solely focusing on the negative. When you see negative aspects, view them in a rational manner and find out if they are indeed facts that are truthful.

Another way to eliminate your negative beliefs is to spend a few minutes every day affirming a **totally different** belief. Five minutes for every new belief is enough if you have a busy day.

You should do this in a quiet place without distractions. Focus on your affirmation and refrain from having any other thoughts. Control your mind so that you do not imagine anything unnecessary. **Concentrate** on the words so you can fully grasp what they mean.

This exercise is effective because it lets you hypnotize yourself lightly. You only focus on one thing. The induced hypnosis causes you to directly move all your beliefs into your subconscious mind.

Some people think that it is their conscious mind that manifests thoughts into reality. What they do **not** know is that it is their subconscious mind that makes this happen. Ideally, you should practice this technique every day for thirty days.

Each day, you will notice a **slight** change until eventually, you will reflect your **new** beliefs.

Chapter 8:

Choosing to Live Without Negativity

Presently after that segment of settling on the correct choice, I trust that we would all be able to concur that a standout amongst the most moral decisions to make in our lives is to dispose of negative considerations and emotions.

Negative reasoning can have a significantly ruinous effect on all parts of our lives. It is never great. When you are drawn into this example of negative reasoning, you are building a jail in your own special personality, holding you as the detainee.

Many individuals attempt separated approaches to break out of their negative idea designs, just to whip themselves and aggravate it. On the off chance that you are battling with negative reasoning, it is conceivable to turn things around and develop internal peace and satisfaction.

In any case, initially, you should submit! You should submit yourself and work hard to expel negative musings and to make an extraordinary level of satisfaction that will remain on until what's to come.

Here are the four keys to break free of pessimism for good:

Perceive your negative thinking patterns

Negative idea designs are tedious, useless considerations. They don't have any genuine reason, but to influence you to have negative feelings, for example, outrage or gloom.

When you figure out how to perceive and distinguish these negative idea designs as they happen, you can begin to define a choice with respect to how to respond.

Move away from negative thinkers

Individuals who are influenced by negative musings feel miserable on the grounds that they don't realize what to do. It might appear as though there are insufficient responses to confront your issues, to enable you to get ready for the future and manage distinctive circumstances.

So how would you travel through the course of days in a way that is astute and honest to goodness without getting inundated in these critical contemplations? All things considered, you should watch your contemplations! To wind up noticeably free of antagonism, you should be made more mindful of your contemplations and what you put into your cerebrum. Begin to spend more regard for what is happening inside your psyche at any gave time.

Particularly, put all your consideration far from negative reasoning that might emerge. In the event that you see something that incenses or stresses you, do your best to fathom it before it turns into an issue! Turn into a mindful spectator of what goes ahead in your internal condition.

Each time your inward mindfulness is conveyed to a negative idea design, it is just assaulting you and convincing you to build up your brain in that capacity. Simply ahead and check whether you can locate these negative musings when they emerge before they pick up excessively compel. In the event that you can't locate these opposite thoughts at to start with, at that point you do have another opportunity to wind up noticeably more mindful of them and to react with positive musings. For instance, when a negative feeling becomes an integral factor, you can redirect your regard for the suppositions of energy that are being produced by such thoughts.

Wind up noticeably mindful

When you have negative considerations, they hover in two headings. The main turn the past; they help you to remember your slips, obstructions, blame, and anything in your life that did not go the way you wished it did. The second is the consistent stress without bounds, and it makes you dreadful of what might possibly happen to yourself or others.

We will find out about this later in this book, however these steady stresses can appear as worry about whether you will accomplish singular objectives or uneasiness about the security of your funds or connections. Or on the other hand possibly you stress over seeming old. To get past these critical idea designs, your mind needs to cast its attention on the past or future.

To end up plainly more completely alert and ready to advance out of this reasoning example of stress, stress, and dread; you should divert your consideration and contemplations into the without further ado. Give your present minute your whole full focus.

Pick constructive thoughts over destructive thoughts

In this way, now that you built up some inward mindfulness you can intentionally choose to change your reasoning with the goal that it is useful as opposed to ruinous. Being sure is a decision. Being negative is additionally a decision.

When you enable yourself to think productively, you enable yourself to be glad when things are either going right or when things are turning out badly. When you accept usefully, you place issues into point of view and for all intents and purposes manage them.

Expelling yourself from antagonism won't occur immediately. You should practice and practice to show signs of improvement at it. The more you build up this mindfulness in your idea designs, the more you can utilize your brain to develop joy. To evacuate mental mess, you just need to step up with regards to expel them and to confer yourself further.

Chapter 9:

Why Declutter Your Mind

One of the most prominent reasons you want to declutter your mind is because it already is playing a negative role in your life. You may be experiencing its effect right now and may want to do something about it.

Most of the available resources we find online and in print when we look for help point out to dealing with the effects of a cluttered mind. This is just like traditional medicine nowadays which uses treatment to deal with the symptoms and not with what is causing the symptoms.

All these pieces of advice have a valid point. But in the end, if you look carefully at the bigger picture, you have to admit that something is missing. No matter how hard you try and succeed in tackling the symptoms that derive from a cluttered mind, you will need to address the central issue you are facing eventually. Your account is slowly and steadily becoming your enemy – the cluttering creeps in, step by step, and only by realizing and reversing this process will you be able to put an end to this spiral of unhappiness.

The benefits derived from dealing with the cause rather than the effects are enormous.

Being Efficient

It is hard not to notice that many of us who try to engage in dealing with problems we're facing in our day-to-day life have limited amounts of energy to spend. We all have to be productive, stay healthy, take care of others that rely on us for their well-being; and at the same time, we have a job or are searching for a job, we are part of a family or a relationship, we have our dreams, desires, needs.

The obvious question arises: is it worth fighting to deal with our problems in such a way that we spend a great deal of time and resources? Does this struggle end eventually? Are we efficient? I'm afraid the honest answer is not a positive one.

Vicious Circle

As I mentioned before, most of the resources that are available for those who strive to achieve happiness in their lives are limited to dealing with the symptoms and not the cause. Moreover, we can observe a pattern that develops. How so?

When we approach an issue that is causing distress by tackling the problem in itself, not only do we lose perspective, but we enter a merry-go-round that takes up a lot of effort and energy and gives us the illusion that we are advancing towards our goal. After we deal with social anxiety by making new friends, the next issue presents itself, for we've spent a lot of money and time and now we felt insecure and stressed over our cost on day-to-day living. If we work more to cover those new expenses, we end up stressed, tired, unable to maintain the relationships we just developed, and hence we get a new form of social anxiety. And even worse, we feel disappointed, and we blame ourselves for that.

Stop. Take a Step Back. Unclutter Your Mind.

We just don't know it could be done with little effort. We have no idea that we stand close to the solution, for we are not examining the correct obstacles. The following chapters will put things in perspective and deal with more detailed aspects of the core concept. For now, keep in mind that there is hardly anyone that can do this on his or her own. Knowledge is power, but at the same time, learning is shared and accumulated not as limited individuals, but as a collective mind that continually improves.

For now, you already feel the answer to the "Why declutter your mind?" question. So let's engage in building up the whole perspective.

When you clear out mental clutter and its symptoms, it can make you feel as if you are **peeling onions**.

Imagine yourself trying to peel off all the layers of the onion so that you can get to the core. This is what decluttering does to your mind. It peels back all your thoughts and ideas. You peel away that which your cluttered thoughts made you believe to get down to your truth.

Everyone has experienced moments of **profound** love, peace, connection, and clarity once all the layers are peeled away. These moments occur when the mind is already clutter-free.

Anyway, before you learn about the exercises that eliminate negative thinking, you should understand the **reason** why you have such thoughts. The following are the most common causes of mental clutter: **Daily Stress**

Too much stress is the **main reason** why so many people feel overwhelmed. In fact, stress caused by information overload, endless options, and physical clutter can trigger various mental health issues, including depression, anxiety, and panic attacks.

Chapter 10:

How Minds Get Cluttered?

S o how do our brains get cluttered? Well, everyone has either clutter accumulated in their minds. In this chapter, we will go over some of the reasons responsible for your brain getting cluttered with negative thoughts. We will tackle ways to prevent cluttering, and we will have a look into one of the most common ways to break the clutter – living a simpler life.

As we already settled, the best way to declutter your mind is to be informed on why your brain is cluttered in the first place. In other words, one of the main reasons people have so much negative energy is because they lack knowledge regarding brain clutter. The majority of the population does not know what confusion is and explains it as something entirely different, blaming either the context, others, or themselves.

The mechanism that clutters our mind is fueled by our uncertainty and social conventions. We live in a society that praises individualism, success, strength, and determination.

When we face obstacles in achieving those, clutter begins to form. But is there a way to prevent it from happening in the first place?

There is good news and bad news. The good news is, being self-aware and having a more relaxed view on things can positively prevent the start of the clustering process. The bad news is, staying confident and comfortable, without stress about small and insignificant things is virtually impossible nowadays.

As we stated before, there are many similarities between the cluttering and a common disease that affects our body. As is the case with the prevalent condition, to prevent, we have to take care of our bodies, to avoid exposing ourselves to evil influences. It's safe to say that the mind follows the same pattern. To prevent clutter, we should not prove ourselves to bad habits, - stress, strong stimuli, overload of info -. Sounds pretty good, but it is tough.

There is no way we could pass through life without interacting with what the present times hold. Unless we choose from the start to isolate ourselves from all that is human and social, becoming monks or taking the ascetic road, it is evident that we have to deal with the challenges and not run away from it.

Going even further with the comparison, a body that wants to prevent illness and disease cannot merely run away from pathogens, isolate from any possible harm. That would achieve the opposite results: our immune system would not be formed, we would become weak and more exposed to getting sick. The same can be applied to our mind. It is never a solution to stay away, and even if some precautions should be taken, living life to the full is the way to go about it. What if all of us choose to get away, to run from each other and isolate ourselves. Hard to imagine, isn't it?

We all know that when falling in love, for example, there is a great deal of risk that love will eventually cause suffering. But that never stopped anyone from searching for love. We know the price, and we are happily ready to pay it. It is part of our existence, so we don't even question it.

The same applies to our mind and the risk of cluttering. Preventing the formation of such clutter is a definite possibility, but acting upon what our immense, complex, and beautiful soul reveals is not debatable. We cannot just put half of our brain on pause. It wouldn't be fair; it wouldn't benefit anyone. So, we can only rely on staying on top of things, being informed and accessing the knowledge that could prevent the creeping in of clutter while at the same time enjoy the vast array of possibilities that derive from it.

Simplifying Your Life to achieve happiness

One of the funniest things related to the act of simplifying our lives is that this is a genuinely complex and complicated endeavor. Paradoxical, right? How can streamline something can be confused? Well, anyone that ever tried this knows exactly how hard and not at all simple it can be.

The new millennium brought into our lives a sense of time that is quickly running away from us, an infinite amount of knowledge that bombards us form some different sources.

Even though it is hard to say these scientific and social achievements are harmful, for it wouldn't be fair, it is entirely appropriate to take a step back and think again. Are those developments that we benefit from today directly connected to our level of happiness? Or, on the contrary, they tend to get in the way of us achieving serenity, joyfulness, and bliss.

Simplifying our lives doesn't mean making it miserable, or cutting ourselves from the delights of the modern society. Instead, it could suggest getting to make a careful selection and filtering of what enriches us. Once we get hold of that, by being honest with ourselves, we could start focusing on that and leaving all the detrimental side-activities outside of our horizon. Unfortunately, this is way easier said than done.

Chapter 11:

Types of Mental Clutter

Mental clutter takes up plenty of space in your brain, making it harder to think through decisions and to enjoy life. If we let it, psychological confusion will move and permanently soak inside our minds, developing a pattern that results in a full absorption of our spiritual energy and health. Our firm belief is that with just a little work, we can all find a way to cleanse our minds and move forward. But first, we must explore the types of mental clutter that exists, so that we become aware and can spot them when they arise. The faster we detect some symptoms, the better:

These are the types of mental clutter that can be incredibly damaging over the long-term:

Worry

Worrying is never good. In fact, it's entirely unproductive. And on some levels, we believe that through worrying we can prevent specific events from unfolding and that we can control our future. However, it's up to us to act in such situations as they arise. The ability of our minds to project itself to the future is a fantastic skill. Just like the possibility to recall the past and learn from it. However, there is a catch: when imagining the future, we do so not by engaging in a rational analysis of facts and info, but we mix emotions, feelings, fear, and uncertainty. Hence, whatever the future holds for us becomes an obstacle in our present moment.

Worry is the most popular form of clutter as it blocks your mind from all sorts of gunk and leaves your brainless room for creativity or problem-solving. As powerful a brain can be, it positively cannot deal with the vast array of difficulties and issues that come up in our ordinary day-to-day road through life. It isn't fair to ask such things of ourselves or our mind.

On the other hand, as high as it may seem at first glance, not worrying enough can also become a problem and make room for clutter. Most of us feel that worrying is detrimental and thus they take refuge in all sorts of escaping methods, either by overlooking the obstacles or by running away from issues and problems into destructive habits, dependencies, abuse of substances or chaotic behavior. We will talk extensively about these problems in a further chapter.

Regret

One of the most visible forms of clutter is through repentance. Now, you must know that there is not a single successful or happy person who has never decided that they've regretted one or more actions or events from their past. We all mourn something, and we all make mistakes. It's part of what makes us human. However, it's up to us to decide whether we will let our mistakes define us or we will learn from them and move forward towards our well-being.

And by the way, we don't have to repeat our mistakes. We all heard that many times. Don't repeat your mistakes, don't engage in actions that follow a destructive pattern, and find the power to change when you've made a mistake. It is still tough to do. It would mean we can both live our lives and also observe ourselves objectively and identify soft spots to work on. Even though it is hard or seems impossible most of the times, it is a substantial possibility, once we get hold of our mind and its tricks. If we acknowledge this fact, we can begin to see the past decisions or recollections that inspire us to feel regret as an opportunity to learn and change ourselves in positive ways. Disappointment is always unhelpful if it does not bring about learning or personal change. We could call it a waste. We can never change the past, but we can always change the future. We can make positive choices today, to prevent future regrettable decisions.

You know how they say there's something good about every evil thing. This is the case of regret; if we keep an open mind, regretting will teach us to finally accept past mistakes as an inevitable part of life and practice the critical art of forgiveness.

Guilt

Life is always about moving forward., But sin keeps us in the past, usually because we ponder about what we should or should not have done in certain situations. As you can imagine, our mind has the infinite ability to develop scenarios. It is a never-ending story. We all have been there. What if I would have said that, maybe I could have changed the outcome. The feeling of guilt is a strong motivator that keeps our mind focused on the past. Always reevaluating, always trying to absolve ourselves of any mistakes we've made. These mechanisms that our brain develop to keep us safe and comfortable can sooner or later have a big price. If not addressed wisely, after a while, guilt can soak into your brain, and it'll be almost impossible to move forward. It is not realistic to say that you'll forget what happened, but it is possible to release the past to live in the present.

Negative Self-talk

Our beliefs regarding ourselves, others, and the world as a whole can profoundly impact what we often say about others, our circumstances, and ourselves. Piece by piece and step by step, what we believe influences what we say and what we say defines how we behave. These belief systems we build for ourselves originate from many experiences we accumulate over our lifetime. One does not merely become a negative self-talker in a day; it takes years for such a mentality to take place, but the reality is not very encouraging. So many of us misinterpret life circumstances, failures, other people's behavior and we tend to take them upon themselves.

But as we all know, negative self-talk is one of the worse mental clutters that can lower our self-esteem and hurt others even if it happens indirectly. When you boldly declare something as being insulting or not very complimenting about yourself, it creeps into your belief system and slowly but surely will manifest later in your life.

Attitude makes the difference! You might recall the famous words of one the most impressive politician of the UK, Winston Churchill, who said: "Attitude is a small thing that makes a big difference." We couldn't agree more. If you go through life thinking that you are not good enough, you will never be good enough. It's that simple. Go through your life being self-aware, but try to figure out all the changes that you need to make. Not what others tell you, but what you feel about that. Write them all down. What are the life changes that you must make, as you think it in your core, in your bones? That's the moment when you establish the foundational point to get you started.

Chapter 12:

Maintaining a decluttered mind

While your body reacts to worry through your sensory system, a few stressors may emerge at certain anticipated circumstances—on your drive to work, when on a gathering with your manager, or even family social events, for instance. Presently to deal with such unsurprising stressors, you either change the current circumstance or change how you respond to it. Whichever alternative you choose to follow up on, dependably think about these four A's: keep away from, adjust, adjust, or acknowledge.

Stay away from unnecessary stress

It may appear to be unfortunate to maintain a strategic distance from a distressing circumstance that should be tended to, however shockingly, there are a few stressors throughout your life that you can wipe out by unadulterated evasion.

Figure out how to state "no" – Know your impediments and stick to them. Regardless of whether it is your expert or individual life, a surefire formula for being worried is the point at which you take more than you can deal with. Separate your "should" and "must" and, when conceivable, say "no" to going up against excessively and remain on it.

Keep away from or avoid individuals who worry you – If somebody is a reliable reason for worry in your life, at that point constrain the measure of time you go through with that individual, or better still end the association with such individual.

Take control of your condition – If the prospect of the nightly news makes you restless, kill the TV. On the off chance that been in rush hour gridlock influences you to tense, take a more drawn out however less-voyaged course. On the off chance that heading off to the market is something you hate and find as a repulsive errand, simply do your shopping for food on the web.

Modify the situation

On the off chance that you have taken a stab at dodging as much as you can an unpleasant circumstance, at that point have a go at circumventing it. Frequently, this may include changing the way you convey and work each day.

Rather than smothering/packaging your sentiments, express it. On the off chance that something or somebody you know is disturbing you, be more decisive and direct to the individual and convey your worries transparently and consciously. On the off chance that you have an exam/meeting to contemplate for and your loquacious flat mate/companion just returned home or came around, say in advance that you just have five minutes to talk. In the event that you don't voice your sentiments, hatred will manufacture, and the pressure will increment since you need to get together with examining.

Compromise on your characters. When you request that somebody change their conduct, be set up to do likewise if require be. In the event that you both will twist no less than a bit, you'll have a decent shot of finding a glad center ground to play on.

Deal with your chance better. Poor time administration we definitely know can cause a great deal of pressure. Be that as it may, in the event that you design and ensuring you don't overextend yourself past your points of confinement, you'll see it less demanding to remain quiet and concentrated on your objectives.

Be more decisive and direct. Try not to assume a lower priority in your own life. Manage each of your issues head-on, and doing your best to expect and in addition anticipate them. Like I referred to prior, in the event that you have an exam to think about for and your glib flat mate just returned home, say in advance that you just have five minutes to talk.

Adjust to the stressor

How your musings are can profoundly affect your feelings of anxiety. Each time you contemplate yourself and the conditions around you, you draw in greater pessimism to yourself, making your body respond as though it were in the throes of a strain filled circumstance. Recapture your feeling of control by changing your desires and your state of mind to unpleasant circumstances.

Reframe issues. Attempt to see distressing circumstances from a more positive point of view. As opposed to raging about a road turned parking lot, take a gander at it as a chance to stop and regroup, tune in to your most loved radio station, or appreciate some alone time.

Take a gander at the 10,000 foot view. Take a full point of view of the upsetting circumstance. Ask yourself how vital it will be over the long haul. Will it matter in a month? A year? Is it worth getting furious about? In the event that the appropriate response is no, center your opportunity and vitality somewhere else.

Ask yourself how key changing it will be over the long haul. Modify your guidelines. Compulsiveness is an essential source through which one can be worried up. Quit setting yourself up for disappointment by requesting flawlessness regardless of your demeanor. Set sensible and achievable norms for yourself as well as other people, and figure out how to approve of "sufficient."

Acknowledge the things you can't change

Go on. Try not to be hesitant to acknowledge the things you can't change which don't appear to be variable.

A few wellsprings of stress are unavoidable. You can't avoid or change stressors, for example, the passing of a friend or family member, the event of a serious disease, or even a national retreat. In these cases, the most ideal approach to adapt to pressure is simply to acknowledge things as they seem to be. Acknowledgment might be troublesome, yet over the long haul, it's simpler than railing against a circumstance you can't change.

Try not to endeavor to control the wild. You are not a Supreme Being. Numerous things that occur in life are route outside our ability to control—especially the conduct and state of mind other individuals depict. Instead of worrying about them and attempting to transform it, concentrate on the things you have control over them, for example, the way you respond to these issues.

Search for the upside in these circumstances. When confronting huge difficulties dissect and take a gander at them as chances to put resources into your self-improvement. In the event that your own poor decisions offered ascend to an upsetting circumstance, contemplate on them and gain from your missteps.

Figure out how to excuse. Acknowledge the way that we live in a blemished world and that individuals are inclined to committing an error. Relinquish all the outrage and feelings of disdain and simply free yourself from negative vitality by pardoning them and proceeding onward with your life.

Practice the specialty of demonstrating appreciation. At the point when stretch is getting you down and is turning you back to front, pause for a minute to think about every one of the things you acknowledge in your life, including your positive qualities and blessings. This straightforward methodology can enable you to keep things in context and influence you to see that you are still on track with your life objectives.

Chapter 13:

Decluttering your thoughts

Before we plunge into the different activities to take out your negative reasoning, it's fundamental initially to comprehend why you have these contemplations. Along these lines, in this area, we'll go more than four reasons for mental mess.

Daily Stress

An exorbitant ammount of stress is the essential reason many individuals feel overpowered by life. Indeed, the weight made by data over-burden, physical mess, and the unlimited decisions required from these things can trigger a variety of emotional wellness issues like summed up nervousness, freeze assaults, and gloom.

Couple this worry with the authentic stresses and worries throughout your life, and you may wind up with rest issues, muscle torment, migraines, chest torment, visit diseases, and stomach and intestinal issue.

The Paradox of Choice

The flexibility of decision, something venerated in free social orders, can have a reducing purpose of return with regards to psychological well-being. Therapist Barry Schwartz authored the adage "mystery of decision," which entireties up his discoveries that expanded decision prompts more huge tension, hesitation, loss of motion, and disappointment. More alternatives may manage the cost of unbiasedly better outcomes, however they won't make you upbeat.

Too Much "Stuff."

Our homes are loaded with garments we never wear, books we won't read, toys that are unused, and devices that don't see the light of day. Our PC inboxes are flooding. Our work areas are jumbled, and our telephones are blazing messages like "You require more stockpiling."

With this consistent stream of data and access to innovation, getting to be plainly mass purchasers of things and information is less demanding than any time in recent memory. At the snap of a catch, we can arrange anything from a book to a speedboat and have it conveyed to our doorstep.

We're filling our homes with things we don't need and filling our chance with a constant flow of tweets, refreshes, articles, blog entries, and feline recordings. Data and stuff are heaping up around us, but then we feel vulnerable to make a move.

The greater part of this unessential stuff and information suck our chance and efficiency, as well as produces responsive, on edge, and negative contemplations.

We regularly feel like we don't have room schedule-wise to clean up in light of the fact that we're excessively bustling devouring new stuff and data. In any case, sooner or later, this hecticness is driving us to mental and enthusiastic depletion. As we process everything coming at us, we investigate, ruminate, and stress ourselves to the limit.

How have we dismissed the qualities and life needs that once kept us adjusted and rational? What would we be able to do about it? We can't backpedal in time and live without innovation. We can't disavow the greater part of our common belonging and abide in a surrender. We need to make sense of an approach to live in this cutting-edge world without losing our rational soundness.

Cleaning up our stuff and curtailing time went through with our advanced gadgets helps dispose of a portion of the tension and negative reasoning. Yet, despite everything we have a lot of motivation to lose all sense of direction in the psychological mess of negative idea, stress, and lament.

We stress over our wellbeing, our occupations, our children, the economy, our connections, what we look like, what other individuals consider us, psychological warfare, governmental issues, torment from the past, and our unusual prospects. Our musings about these things influence us to endure and undermine the joy we could encounter at this moment on the off chance that we didn't have that consistent voice in our heads mixing things up.

The Negativity Bias

The human sensory system has been advancing for 600 million years, yet despite everything it reacts the same as our initial human progenitors who confronted hazardous circumstances all the time and required simply to survive.

Meditation

You don't need to be a Buddhist, a spiritualist, or a precious stone conveying ex-radical to rehearse contemplation. You can have a place with any profound or religious confidence or have no religious association at all to receive the rewards of reflection and utilize it as an instrument for cleaning up your psyche.

In the event that you've never drilled contemplation or you're not acquainted with it, you may be put off by sitting discreetly in the lotus position and purging your psyche. In any case, don't let the banalities about pondering cavern inhabitants keep you from try it attempt.

Reflection has been polished for a huge number of years and begins in antiquated Buddhist,

Hindu, and Chinese customs. There are many styles of thoughtful practices, however most strategies start with similar advances—sitting unobtrusively, concentrating consideration on your breath, and expelling any diversions that come your direction.

The objective of contemplation changes relying upon the kind of reflection hone and the coveted result of the meditator. For our motivations here, we propose contemplation as an instrument to enable you to prepare your brain and control your musings, both when you are sitting in reflection and when you aren't.

The advantages of reflecting convert into your every day life, helping you control stress and overthinking, and giving a large group of medical advantages that we'll examine underneath.

The way to discovering fulfillment with contemplation only is to hone. By making a day by day responsibility regarding reflection, you will enhance your abilities and find how the psychological, physical, and enthusiastic advantages increment after some time.

Here is a basic 11-step process you can use to manufacture the contemplation propensity:

Select a tranquil, quiet space for your contemplation hone where you can close the way to be totally alone.

Decide a particular time of day for your training. In the event that you've started a profound breathing practice, you can utilize this as your trigger (and beginning stage) for your new contemplation propensity. Or on the other hand you can pick another trigger and work on ruminating at some other time of day.

Choose whether you need to reflect sitting on a cushion on the floor or in a straight-back seat or couch. Make an effort not to lean back as you think about, since you may nod off.

Evacuate all diversions and kill every single advanced gadget or different gadgets that make commotion. Expel pets from the room.

Set a clock for 10 minutes.

Sit easily either in a seat or leg over leg on the floor with a pad. Keep your spine erect and your hands resting delicately in your lap.

Close your eyes, or keep them open with a descending centered look, at that point take a couple of profound purifying breaths through your nose—we suggest three or four breaths at any given moment.

Bit by bit wind up noticeably mindful of your relaxing. Notice the air moving in and out through your nostrils and the ascent and fall of your chest and stomach area. Enable your breaths to fall into place easily, without compelling them.

Concentrate on the impression of breathing, maybe even rationally thinking "in" as you breathe in and "out" as you breathe out.

Your musings will meander a great deal first and foremost. Each time they do, tenderly let them go and after that arrival your thoughtfulness regarding the impression of relaxing.

Try not to judge yourself for having nosy contemplations. That is only your "monkey mind" attempting to assume control. Just lead your brain back to concentrated consideration on relaxing. You may need to do this dozen of times at first.

As you concentrate on breathing, you'll likely notice different recognitions and sensations like sounds, physical inconvenience, feelings, and so forth. Simply advise these as they emerge in your mindfulness, and afterward tenderly come back to the energy of relaxing.

You will likely progressively turn into the observer to all sounds, sensations, feelings, and contemplations as they emerge and pass away. View them just as you are watching them from a separation without judgment or private remark.

As opposed to your mind taking control and fleeing at whatever point an idea or diversion happens, you in the long run acquire and more energy of your record and your capacity to divert it back to the present.

At the outset, you'll feel you're in a steady fight with your monkey mind. In any case, with training, you won't have to divert your considerations dependably. Considerations start to drop away normally, and your record opens up to the tremendous stillness and immensity of simply being available. This is a really tranquil, fulfilling knowledge.

Contemplation experts allude to this space of stillness as the "hole"— the noiseless space between musings. At in the first place, the hole is extremely tight, and it's hard to stay there for more than a couple of nanoseconds. As you turn into a more honed meditator, you'll discover the hole opens more extensive and all the more as often as possible, and you can rest in it for more expanded timeframes.

You can encounter a concise snapshot of the space between contemplations by attempting this activity: Close your eyes and start to see your considerations. Just watch them travel every which way for a couple of moments. At that point make the inquiry, "Where will my next idea originate from?" Stop and sit tight for the appropriate response. You may see there's a short hole in your reasoning while you anticipate the answer.

Chapter 14:

Importance of Decluttering Distractions that Cause stress and Anxiety

W hen you take yourself off the grid, you remove the distractions that you encounter on a daily basis. These are the ones that **cause** your stress, fears, frustrations, and anger. When you wrestle with life, whether in your work, family, school, or religion, you should get rid of all the external influences that contribute to your worries and anxiety.

Eliminating the Distraction

Many people have the **desire** to reduce distractions, but they are not able to do it because they are full of **excuses**. Their reasoning may not even be justified. If you are one of these people, your purpose may not have your best intentions in mind and at heart.

"If I lose my mobile phone service, an emergency may happen, and I won't be able to get in touch with anybody."

"What if somebody needed to get a hold of me?"

"If I receive an e-mail on the weekend, I have to answer it. Otherwise, my boss will think that I am not working."

"I feel bored when there is nothing for me to do."

"I enjoy having a busy week and having lots of tasks to accomplish."

"I might miss out on certain things."

It can be challenging to get rid of distractions at first. You will always find a way to make an excuse. However, once you get over the **initial** heartbreak of disconnecting, you will realize that the circumstances are not that bad.

Why Is It Important to Declutter the Distractions that Cause You to Be Anxious?

Getting Rid of Distractions Helps You Slow Down. Your body is not the only thing that moves a lot; your mind does too. You exhaust your mind thinking about your daily chores and tasks. The distractions around you make matters worse by draining your account further. What you can do to rejuvenate your mind is rejuvenated your body. You need to take a break from **all** the action to avoid **breaking down**.

Getting Rid of Distractions Help You Focus on One Thing at a Time. When there isn't **anything** that distracts you, it becomes easier to concentrate on what is right in front of you. This could be anything, from spending time with your family and friends to writing a book to completing a project. When there is no distraction, you can devote all your intentions and efforts to **one thing** at a time.

Getting Rid of Distractions Allows You to Put Everything Into Perspective. Not everything is a big deal. Recognize the fact that there are **times** when you tend to make significant issues out of small problems. You add unnecessary stress to your day, which is why you feel even more anxious. When you get rid of **distractions**, you can see life for what it is rather than what you make it out to be.

Chapter 15:

Investing in Yourself

What is investing in yourself?

What strikes a chord when you hear the word contributing? Does it mean, putting your cash in protection, common supports, money markets or even high return speculations? Other individuals may just consider spending when they are going to bite the dust, and they haven't left anything for their posterity.

Many individuals even put vigorously in wellbeing supplements, fitness coaches and beauticians to influence themselves to live more, more advantageous or additionally look more youthful! Envision the promoting spending plan for magnificence organizations these days.

The most fundamental and No.1 run is to "Put resources into Yourself. In the event that you don't, who else will?

Your folks will just put resources into your instruction until the point when you leave school. Yet, that is only the necessities and does not show you significant lessons about money related proficiency.

Would you rely upon schools or colleges to show you how to profit? Most schools just show you aptitudes so you can gain cash working for other individuals. What about business college? Truly, if business speakers are such specialists at business, why are despite everything they addressing there as opposed to making a fortune in business wanders?

Would your supervisor show you how to prevail in business with the goal that one day, you will be in his position?

You and just you must be sufficiently proactive to assume that liability.

When you put resources into yourself, it implies going up against the significance of instructing yourself. Try not to trust that training is restricted to the scholarly or specialized sense, however they are important abilities to be produced throughout everyday life. Our insight does not and ought not stop at school.

For most working grown-ups, their training enters an impediment arrange after they leave school. They quit learning, and in this manner they quit developing.

We realize that IQ is critical right? In any case, for what reason aren't the most keen individuals on the planet the wealthiest individuals on the planet? There are numerous bookkeepers and money related organizers hurrying to their autos each night endeavoring to beat the after work movement! They are not rich!

So how is putting resources into yourself done?

Wander off in fantasy land a bit.

What have you generally needed to attempt? Presently's an ideal opportunity to plan exactly that — whatever it is. Skydive, get up a half hour early consistently to compose that Great American Novel, visit a nearby fascination that you've generally been interested about however never made an appearance at — whatever.

Setting aside the opportunity to accomplish something that you've for a long while been itching to do is a method for demonstrating to yourself that YOU are essential. You'll feel more fiery and simply better all in all. Like that old business says, "you're justified, despite all the trouble!".

Take in another ability.

Truly, this could include taking a class or taking in another aptitude. Be that as it may, it could likewise mean perusing up regarding a matter utilizing books from the library, or downloading a French podcast and rehearsing each day. Or on the other hand it could mean joining a weaving club for fledglings and adapting together in a gathering. Hell, it could even propose currently attempting to enhance your score in the most recent cell phone amusement.

The fact of the matter is to explore new territory that requires practice and exertion. Practicing your mind helps keep it sharp, and makes life a mess all the more intriguing.

Get over an old hindrance.

We as a whole have things that are keeping us down, shielding us from being the general population we truly could be in the event that we worked through an issue. Possibly you stress constantly or are unbelievably timid yet long to have companions. Or then again maybe your financial records is overdrawn constantly and you and your mate are continually battling for cash.

It's the ideal opportunity for a change. Get directing, get treatment, get whatever it takes to get over that old hindrance and move past it. It's one venture that will be WELL justified, despite all the trouble.

Make sound propensities.

Eat well, get enough rest, and exercise every day. Sound propensities give you the vitality to DO the things you need to do, instead of being keep running down and debilitated. There's in no way like dealing with yourself to enhance the nature of your life.

Offer yourself a reprieve.

At long last, a standout amongst the most disregarded approaches to put resources into yourself is simply to offer yourself a reprieve every once in a while. In case you're so finished booked that you're generally worried from hurrying all over, drop something. You don't have to do everything. We as a whole need breaks, and you are no special case. Back rubs are extraordinary, however just doing nothing is a phenomenal break as well. At the point when was the last time you booked a do-nothing day?

The exact opposite thing staying after you start perusing, tuning in and partner is to execute all that you have learned. Try not to give these assignments a chance to threaten you and begin applying with extra special care. Similarly as Rome wasn't worked in a day, it will set aside the opportunity to aggregate information and follow up on it. Be that as it may, it is a basic advance in light of the fact that no experience will consistently bring any outcome unless it is followed up on. To know and not to do isn't to know!

Thus, begin now and put resources into yourself, build up the fundamental aptitudes for progress, and acquire the most noteworthy return you will ever get. Here's to your prosperity!

Instructions to Achieve What You Want in Life

On the off chance that you have a fantasy, a conspicuous and daring objective that you need to accomplish, you will require an arrangement of fitting abilities. You can discover a huge number of tips regarding this matter, yet no place else will you see a basic rundown of 2-3 most vital abilities which when organized, will ensure your coveted outcome. Why would that be? Since not very many think about it and those that do – well they need to keep it a mystery or offer it with few.

I have been ordering this learning a little bit at a time all through as long as I can remember, continually applying these basic yet hugely powerful standards and I might want to leave this experience for descendants and each one of the individuals who will tune in. It is the most satisfying and exceptional feeling one can accomplish, to have the capacity to take an interest in the prosperity of his colleagues. I don't have anything to stow away on the grounds that exclusive a couple of you will have the capacity to tune in and apply these standards, lamentably. Then again, the way that you try to secure information places you in a flawless place. As hard as it is to accept, there are not all that many like you.

Keep in mind that your arrangement of convictions or what you have confidence in is your most fantastic guide throughout everyday life. All that you think in turns into your existence, so it is crucial to think inaccurate standards, in something that is for sure evident. Greater part of individuals today think in made up things without acknowledging it. They battle devils and ghosts. In this manner, they can never control their lives. Search for reality, and you will discover it! Try not to enable anybody to mentally program you, and by somebody, I mean merchants, government officials, religious enthusiasts thus called "researchers." Today it has turned out to be so normal to confide in science, allude to logical research albeit present day researchers have made more "evil spirits" than any alchemists or voodoo men. Get your declaration of everything that you're learning and manufacture your arrangement of convictions in light of such establishments.

Be consistent with your wants

SECOND, no less of a vital expertise is to know precisely what you need out of life. Figure out what you need in the first place, second, et cetera. What cost would you say you will pay? You either pay in advance, for instance by venturing out of your customary range of familiarity, with your opportunity and diligent work, or you pay later, for example by losing your flexibility, companions, family, wellbeing or with add up to frustration throughout everyday life. Continuously think about the results! On the off chance that you don't recognize what you need out of life, it will be loaded with episodes, and not extremely lovely ones at that. In this way, design your life or else somebody will set it up for you! The best technique for arranging is to record it on paper. Dreams, preponderances, supplications, reflections, representations – THESE are imperative.

The ability to think big, creatively and at the same time to be able to focus on a goal is not an easy task. Therefore, learning is required. For starters, you would need to master specific thinking tools – concentration, visualization and mind-mapping is the necessary minimum. Planning on paper and not just in your head using a mind map allows you to learn and to think efficiently, intelligently, and so fast that no other genius of the past can ever compare.

Never stop. Affirm and visualize.

FOURTH, an essential skill for achieving goals is to learn about strengths in yourself and discard any and all excuses and persevere to the end! By using the third power described above (the cycle of achievement) and observing how one comes up with all kinds of excuses not to do anything, learn to discard such explanations and persevere to the end. Affirmations and visualizations can help here.

Of course, this isn't a complete list of skills but is sufficient to achieve practically any realistic goal. The ability to communicate effectively can also be added to this list although for some it is one of the innate qualities or is developed within the family. If you were not gifted in this area, self-education and knowledge of the essential laws of communication could help you.

The Golden Rule

One of those laws is so called the Golden Rule: "Do unto others as you would have them do unto you." You just need to remember that it is not only a mere wish or a good rule of behavior in society, but it is one of the most harsh laws of the universe. Because people will always treat you the way, you treat them. Lying, deceit, hypocrisy, violence, stealing, poverty and sickness in your life are the result of your dishonesty, disrespect, fraud, greed, and hatred for others. In the same respect, joy, health, abundance, success, and happiness is the result of your love and selfless service to others. This type of service is the key to prosperity, personal growth, and happiness. Make it your habit. Serve everyone you meet – at home, at work, at play.

Service, however, doesn't mean doing their job instead of them. Make service part of your mental attitude. Whatever you do, don't do it because you must, not out of obligation, not for money or any future benefit. Do it because of the joyful desire to serve those you love, which means virtually everyone you meet. Such mental attitude on its own can fill your life with prosperity and love. Just remember that the most excellent source of love is YOU!

Minimalist Living

In this section, we will go over why you might want to consider becoming a minimalist and the many benefits that derive from it. Of course, this entire book is about living the minimalist lifestyle and to be therefore able to declutter your mind for the best.

Minimalism can be defined merely as a way to put a stop to the greed of the world around us. It's the opposite of every advertisement we see plastered on the radio, TV or the web. We live in a society that prides itself on the accumulation of stuff; we are fed up with consumerism, obsess about material possessions, accumulating debt, dwelling on distractions and never-ending noise. What we don't seem to have is any meaning left in our world as we know it.

By adopting a minimalist lifestyle, you can start by throwing out what you don't need to focus on what you do need. I know firsthand how little we need to survive. I was fortunate enough to live in a van for four months while traveling throughout Australia. This experience taught me many valuable lessons about what matters and how little we need from all this stuff we surround ourselves with.

Less is more

Living a minimalist lifestyle is all about reducing what can be reduced. There are a few obvious benefits such as less cleaning and stress, a more organized household, and more money to be found, but there are also a few broad, life-changing benefits. What we don't usually realize is that when we reduce, we reduce a lot more than just stuff. If anything, the constant struggle of accumulating more and more things is a particular path to mind cluttering. Studies have shown that after a certain level of satisfaction is achieved when buying something; there is an absolute decrease in satisfaction that eventually tends to get to zero. The economists call it marginal satisfaction. The most common example they use to explain this concept is easy to grasp: think about the most fantastic cake you can imagine. Before you have it, you are susceptible to manifest a strong desire to eat that cake. After the first bite, you feel a great deal of satisfaction. The second taste can keep a high level of comfort but at some point the pleasure you feel from eating the cake slowly decreases. When you buy the same cake for the second time, a much lower degree of satisfaction is to be expected. The same happens with all possessions, no matter the origin.

The power of advertising makes it, so it is almost impossible for an individual to resist the urge of buying more and more things. They sell the projected satisfaction you will feel, but they never follow-up after you buy the product.

Make space for what's vital

When we cleanse our garbage drawers and storage rooms, we make space, and we likewise interface with an outright peace. In the event that I would pick a correlation, the one that comes close by, and that I likewise alluded to in the early on section of this book is the carousel. The jumbling wonders happen when we neglect to oppose the powerful stream of our general public, and we take part in this extreme and exhausting beat of steady purchasing with less and less fulfillment and point of view. In the event that we prepare for what is essential, accepting we discharge what that is, we lose that claustrophobic inclination, and we can inhale once more. Make place to top off our lives with importance rather than stuff is a standout amongst the most proficient approaches to clean up and put a conclusion to self-depletion.

More flexibility

The steady and nonstop collection of stuff resembles a stay; it secures us and indicates the weight we feel consistently. Envision you labor for three months and spare cash to purchase a costly device. Subsequent to getting a charge out of it for quite a while, not exclusively does the fulfillment you get from it diminishes, yet there's another advancement that emerges – we get connected to that protest, and we gradually however most likely build up the dread of losing it. On the off chance that we are straightforward, we understand that we are constantly frightened of losing our 'stuff.' Manage to release it, and you will encounter opportunity more than ever: flexibility from voracity, obligation, fixation and workaholic behavior. Much more thus, odds are the jumbling can't sneak in that effectively.

Concentrate on wellbeing and pastimes

When you invest less energy at Home Depot attempting unsuccessfully to stay aware of the Joneses, you make an opening to do the things you adore, things that you never appeared to have time for. Also, the illustrations are such a large number of we could compose a completely new book just by assembling cases of dawdled doing fantastically insignificant things. We as a whole have been there, furtively wishing the 24 hour day would change into a 48 hour one, only for us, without any other person to know. In any case, at that point, if that would turn out to be valid, who could ensure that we wouldn't at present invest all the energy we have done a wide range of unimportant things that, at most, give us the dream that we can rest easy.

Everybody is continually saying they don't have enough time, yet what number of individuals stop and take a gander at what they are investing their energy doing? It's to some degree clever, yet it appears that there is no time just to wrap up. You could appreciate a day with your children, hitting up the rec center, rehearsing yoga, perusing a decent book or voyaging. Whatever it is that you cherish you could do, however rather you are stuck at Sears looking for more stuff. Disappointing, would it say it isn't?

Concentrate Less on material belonging

All the stuff we encircle ourselves with is just a diversion, and we are filling a void. Cash can't purchase satisfaction; we as a whole know the colloquialism. In any case, it can purchase comfort. After the underlying delight is fulfilled, that is the place our fixation on cash should end. Tragically, that is decisively where everything starts, for it is for the most part an exemplary instance of getting tied up with a fanciful solace. How about we understand this from with a better point of view. Envision you are eager. At that point, envision your mind believes that you ate, however your body doesn't get the nourishing substances it needs. For quite a while, in light of the dream that happens inside your psyche, you don't feel hungry any longer.

After that hallucination breaks, and they all do in the long run, do you feel hungrier than some time recently, as well as chances are you now feel wiped out, depleted, and drained? The same occurs with the deceptive filling of the void a considerable lot of us think.

It's hard not to get reserved into the consumerism trap. I additionally require steady updates that it's every one of the misguided feeling of joy. I have minutes when I appreciate stuff, however I additionally perceive that I needn't bother with them,

We are barraged by the media displaying guarantees of satisfaction through material measures. Their instruments and abilities are significantly further developed than we might suspect they are. Furthermore, morals isn't the solid purpose of this area. In this manner, it's no big surprise we battle each day. The best counsel is to oppose those desires, despite the fact that it appears to be hard. In the event that we as a whole understand this is a vacant way that won't make us cheerful, we have a decent beginning stage.

More significant serenity

When we stick to material belonging, we make pressure since we are constantly perplexed of losing these things. By rearranging your life, you can lose your connection to these things and at last make a quiet, serene personality.

The less things you need to stress over, the more peace you have, and it's as straightforward as that.

More joy

While cleaning up your brain and your whole life, joy normally comes since you float towards the things that issue most. From being this last apparently inaccessible objective, satisfaction changes into an undeniable conclusion. You see the false guarantees that live in all the messiness, and you have an inclination that you have at last broken the shield against life's actual substance.

You will likewise discover satisfaction in being more productive, you will see focus by having refocused your needs, and you will see happiness by appreciating backing off your pace and cadence.

Less dread of disappointment

When you take a gander at Buddhist priests, they have no uncertainty, and they have no uncertainty since they don't have anything to lose, nor to pick up, so far as that is concerned

In whatever you wish to seek after you can exceed expectations on the off chance that you aren't tormented with the dread of losing all your common belonging. Clearly, you have to find a way to put a rooftop over your head, yet in addition realize that you have little to fear aside from fear itself. The jumbling, as we settled as of now, feast upon our worry, and there are few to no psychological systems that could help us in such manner. What helps, as we continue expressing all through the book, is learning, mindfulness, and point of view. In the event that anything, valor is developed by getting to this specific know-how and never releasing it.

More certainty

The whole moderate way of life advances singularity and confidence. By the by, it doesn't energize independence, self-centeredness, the expansion of one's sense of self. These days, an ever-increasing number of individuals get captured in this example that builds up the sense of self and thinks little of others. Genuine trust in yourself has nothing to do with decreasing others. Despite what might be expected. As expressed unmistakably in a past section of this book, helping other people and attempting to benefit them to the best of your capacities is simply the way certainty. This accepted exertion of situating towards others will make you more sure about your quest for bliss.

Keep, toss, offer, give.

Experience your closet, your books, even your recollections and settle on this: what you're keeping, what you're discarding, what you're offering, and what you're giving.

Garments, for instance, any thing that hasn't been worn for a long time, ought to go into one of the classifications said above.

Endeavor to locate a higher reason for this activity, something that will additionally persuade you. The demonstration of providing for the ones that are not as lucky, as a gift to philanthropy is the best choice out there.

Enter second-hand bunches on the web, possibly compose a carport deal for every one of your companions. On the off chance that the thing is too out designed, complete a correct deed and give it to somebody who has some expertise in making new, useful garments for those in require from the material of old garments.

After you dispose of the garments you don't wear, sort out your closet and bode well upbeat by appreciating the outcome – it is at long last the finish of the ceaseless tumult in your storage room.

You never thought it was conceivable, did you?

As the case presents itself, one of the indications of psyche jumbling that I find more frequently than I might want to concede is this: individuals get sincerely connected to things. The idea of enthusiastic esteem is orbiting the way we connect a few items with what they look like, or with what sort of memory it influences us to review.

A standout amongst the most charming yet commonsense answers for this issue introduced itself to me while having a discussion about this subject with an old man I met at a craftsmanship presentation, numerous years back. He was recording words like what labels or watchwords are, these days, on the web, in his note pad.

At the point when, sooner or later, I enquired him about his training, he revealed to me that he makes recollections by affiliation. Maybe a couple words for each work of art he loved, maybe a couple words for each workmanship question he adored. He said this is his one of a kind method for following his enthusiasm for gathering stunning bits of craftsmanship.

I was dazed by his vision, and I would always remember his note pad which appeared to be amazingly important.

Discover your direction

There are numerous manners by which you could, inevitably, begin strolling the way to a moderate living style. One thing is certain, however: as you do it, the beneficial outcome it has at the forefront of your thoughts increments exponentially. A little space toward the start is gradually however clearly going to end up plainly a gigantic arrangement of opportunity at last.

Being free from the oppression of belonging is a flat out way to your mind's cleaning up process, and hence I ask everybody to in any event attempt this undertaking to see

Conclusion

Thank you again for purchasing this book!

I hope this book was able to teach you the habits, actions, and mindsets you can use beat stress and clean up the mental clutter that might be holding you back from being more focused and mindful.

The next step is to put into practice what you read in this book because you'll find that this book is full of exercises that can have an immediate, positive impact on your mindset.

In other words, you should find a "quick win" that will have an immediate impact on your life.

Thank you and good luck!

MINIMALISM

---- ❧❧❧❧ ----

THE PRACTICAL MINIMALIST STRATEGIES TO SIMPLIFY YOUR HOME AND LIFE

CHLOE S

Contents

Introduction

I want to thank you and congratulate you for purchasing the book, *"MINIMALISM: THE PRACTICAL MINIMALIST STRATEGIES TO SIMPLIFY YOUR HOME AND LIFE"*.

This book contains proven steps and strategies on how to filter and shed the excess stuff and live your life with purpose. The philosophy of minimalism can be applied to any part of your life: what you own, what you do for work, what you put on your calendar, and how you relate to and connect with other people.

Minimalism is not about living in a tiny home and never owning more than 100 things (though you can certainly do that). To live as a minimalist does not mean you have to give up modern conveniences. There is one guiding principle for deciding what stays and what goes: figure out what brings value and purpose to your life and let go of the rest.

Applying this principle is not a one-size-fits-all approach. Each of us—individuals, couples, and families—will use this policy for our particular season and situation. We will have different answers to the question of what brings value and purpose. You are reading this book because of your interest in minimalism. You also probably suspect that our culture's intense pursuit of having more and doing more doesn't lead to lasting happiness. Like me, you want to set about discovering how less means more in your life.

Minimalism helps you reassess your priorities so that you can identify and strip away the excess that doesn't line up with what you want. Although the journey often starts with removing physical clutter, it also leads you to let go of the clutter from your heart and soul. It brings awareness to the void in your life that you're trying to fill with things that will not fill it, at least not for very long.

Thanks again for purchasing this book, I hope you enjoy it!

or abuse of any policies, processes, or directions contained within is the solitary and utter responsibility of the recipient reader. Under no circumstances will any legal responsibility or blame be held against the publisher for any reparation, damages, or monetary loss due to the information herein, either directly or indirectly.

Respective authors own all copyrights not held by the publisher.

The information herein is offered for informational purposes solely, and is universal as so. The presentation of the information is without contract or any type of guarantee assurance.

The trademarks that are used are without any consent, and the publication of the trademark is without permission or backing by the trademark owner. All trademarks and brands within this book are for clarifying purposes only and are the owned by the owners themselves, not affiliated with this document.

Chapter 1:

An overview of minimalism

History of Minimalism

The minimalist movement was one that began in 1960's America in the art world in response to an art culture that had become cluttered and overblown. Minimalist artists of the time considered that the overuse of symbolism and metaphors in art had become excessive and reacted by creating a new form of art which focused on the materials of art, rather than the message.

For example, instead of painting canvases overloaded with hidden meanings and symbols, the minimalist might create a sculpture from a discarded piece of pottery or paint a portrait of a lone red square. The point was to make a return from the endless searching for meaning through motifs in art and instead embrace the simplicity of the essence of art; its materials and raw form.

The point was to create works with no concealed references to politics, history, current events or hot topics, but to create jobs which were beautiful in their simplicity simply.

Music followed suit. A 1964 composition by American composer Terry Riley named merely In C is widely considered the first arrangement of a minimalist music piece. As in the art world, music compositions had become overloaded with unnecessary instruments and layers, creating music that was ultimately unpleasant to listen to and an assault on the senses. The minimalist movement in music was a return to more straightforward harmonies with fewer instruments that allowed the listener to appreciate every note.

Fashion, too, embraced the movement. Minimalist fashion follows the same rules as in art and music; namely rejecting any design which is over-complicated or covered in any logos or images which refer to any subject and draw attention away from the everyday and straightforward form of the garment itself. Many people think of minimalist fashion to mean wearing nothing but all black or all white and having no accessories, but real minimalist style goes even further than this, with designs that may be very complex to tailor being considered minimalist because ultimately, when worn, they appear to have streamlined, simplistic forms.

Alternatively, minimalist fashion can seem bizarre as it may go so far as to even reject the form of the body itself and therefore garments can be deliberately designed to draw attention away from the figure of the wearer.

Of course, after the minimalist movement was adopted in the cultural spheres of art, music, and fashion, it was embraced by interior designers all over the world. Minimalism in interior design evolved a little later than minimalism for music, art, and fashion, but has become a favorite style across the globe.

The fundamental principle of minimalist interior design is 'less is more' and has been influenced by styles from homes all over the world, especially from interior design styles in Japan. Minimalist homes are devoid of clutter and use color sparingly and in a block rather than using patterned wallpapers or murals, for example.

While interior design embraced minimalism in the twentieth-century, the architecture of buildings was becoming minimalist in design from as early as the 1920's. Minimalist structures often use geometric shapes such as domes and triangles in their design and materials such as glass and steel to prevent buildings from being over-stimulating to the eye.

In the modern world, minimalism can be seen in the designs of technological devices, such as streamlined laptops and TVs with no visible buttons or controls. Over the last century, minimalism has been adopted in some form in every visual culture.

However, the movement has grown from there, and there are people today who consider minimalism not to be merely an aesthetic ideology, but a way of life. The philosophy of a minimalist lifestyle is to live without all the non-essentials in life, such as excessive material belongings and flashy cars and homes.

Now, the minimalist lifestyle may not have originated directly from the visual cultures we have spoken about, but the ideals are primarily the same, and often the minimalist visual cultures come hand in hand with a minimalist lifestyle as a whole. Some people would say that their minimalist's belief stem, preferably, from a Zen or Buddhist approach to life, whereby attachment to material possessions is obstacles to true happiness.

For others, an excess of possessions or the demand of household bills and chores became detrimental to the lifestyle they truly desired; lives that are full of travel and easy mobility. For these people, material possessions act as an anchor to tie them down and prevent them from freely moving through life. For others still, a minimalist life is sister to green living, whereby the real intent is to reduce our impact on the earth by becoming less reliant on consumerist goods.

What is Minimalism?

To find out if the minimalist lifestyle is for you, ask yourself these critical questions:

- Would I be able to live without so many material possessions?

Chapter 1: An overview of minimalism

- Would my life improve if I owned less material things?

- How would reducing the clutter in my physical and mental space affect me and those around me?

How you answer these questions will show you the path towards creating a minimalist lifestyle. In a shopping-obsessed, materialistic society, is it possible to live well, be happy and resist the need to buy things you don't need?

I'd say yes! I'm going to show you exactly how. How you can enjoy life, reach inner peace and lead a fulfilled happy life – with fewer material belongings, less mind-clutter and less harmful energy.

This book is divided into several parts that represent different areas of life. Under every section, you'll find chapters or sub-categories with real-life advice related to the region in question.

To help you, even more, we compiled a month's worth of small, yet meaningful steps for living a minimalist life. They are all simple, easy and effortless things you can do to try out if this lifestyle suits you; also, they're things that many minimalist people do every day in all areas of their lives.

Minimalism is a mindful practice. It is why we coined the phrase, 'The Mindful Minimalist.' It's about being grateful for what you own, knowing what you need (which is different from what you want) and using it to clear your mind, improve your relationships, and thrive on simple things rather than drown in possessions. Ultimately, it's about being happy with who you are and what you have now.

I invite you to read this book apply the advice you'll find here as you see best.

Why Choose Minimalism?

Now that we explained the primary purpose of minimalism, you're probably curious about why you should choose the minimalist lifestyle. You're probably inclined to ask more questions:

- What good will it do for my loved ones and me?

Chapter 1: An overview of minimalism

- Will I be happier if I decide to become a minimalist?

- Isn't it a bit radical to suddenly change my life and get out of my comfort zone?

- Will I be able to get used to spending/having less?

Let us try and answer them for you.

Minimalism isn't living in a sterile, dull, monotone environment. In fact, it is the opposite. The way you create your minimalist life depends entirely on you and your priorities. The underlying philosophy behind minimalism is to bring you more financial, emotional, material, and physical clarity and freedom. When you make space for the truly relevant things and people in your life, all other areas will start to follow as well.

People who are not familiar with the minimalist lifestyle can sometimes view it as radical or fringe. But once you realize and become aware that you don't need excess material things to make you fulfilled and happy, it's not even close to radical. It's simplicity. It's the ability to live a simple life and find meaning and joy in the things that you prioritize.

Some people embrace change, and their transition to a minimalist lifestyle is easy, and they get used to it quickly. There are also people whose adjustment to change takes time and effort. So, the answer to this question is something you'd have to estimate according to your personality. If this lifestyle suits you and you feel lighter and better because of it, you're sure to get used to it and enjoy it.

Here are some key reasons to embrace minimalism:

- You will no longer be owned by your possessions. Instead, you'll learn how to select which ones are necessary and essential and which are just mere clutter;

- You'll gain a sense of freedom and liberation from the pressures of "modern" life. You'll understand that success comes from within – from your feeling of fulfillment and not from having an enormous home, several cars, comfortable clothes, and jewelry or social status.

- You'll spend less money. And that's a good thing. Spending less on things you don't need means saving pay for things you do need. And that's called financial freedom.

- You'll feel more productive. Decluttering your mind, life and home, as well as your working space, can contribute significantly to productivity. All the energy that comes with an over-stuffed place will go away, and new, fresh one will take its place. It'll bring you positivity, fresh ideas and a feeling of openness and will-power.

- You'll learn not to get attached emotionally to material objects. Instead, use that energy to connect with the people you love. That's way better for your well-being than any item you'd buy.

- The reduction is the keyword when adopting a minimalist lifestyle. Expect to reduce significantly the number of items that you and your family own. These will be items that are not essential for surviving and living – mostly; they're items that you bought as an impulse purchase, things you keep "just in case" you ever need them, things you buy in bulk so that you're never out of something and basically, anything extra. This creates room for air, energy and essential elements.

- You'll have more time to devote to your hobbies, family, and health. This is one of the best benefits of the minimalist lifestyle – your time will be occupied by the things and people you love instead of struggling to buy more things that you don't need. Objects can't love you back – people can.

- The minimalist lifestyle inevitably brings peace. However, some people fear the future because they're afraid that if they don't have something, they won't be happy, they'll suffer, or they'll end up miserable. Minimalism is not poverty. It's just living a simple life. Money in the bank is always better than having no money and lots of possessions.

- Minimalism doesn't restrict having things. It just teaches you to shop more substantially. Spending less (or not at all) on unworthy items leaves you more money for things that'll bring value and positive change into your life.

When all benefits combine, the result is a happier, more fulfilled and more meaningful life. To sum up, the overall philosophy of Minimalism is in approaching your way of life and how you think about the physical things you own. Do the material attributes you hold in your life empower you to live out your dreams or are they restricting your time and energy? Is the maintenance, organization, and storage of your items giving your more time or less? Let the Minimalist philosophy inspire you in this journey of being more and having less.

The transformation of your current life to a minimalistic lifestyle can seem slightly daunting. This is because you're about to make a significant change in habits, consumption, finances, and your overall life. Though you know this difference is for the better, you're still scared of how it will all turn out.

Fear of the future and how your life will unfold is normal. You think you'll have less, when in fact, you'll have enough. If you've never experienced the minimalist lifestyle firsthand, this is probably your primary concern.

To build a minimalist life, first, you need to think like a minimalist. To do that, you're going to need to simplify your mindset, your ambitions, emotions, and desires. Declutter your mind to make space for new, positive thoughts and empowering mindsets. Then, you can go on and plan your minimalist home, room decor, food, work, *etc.*

Your mind creates your life. It establishes the "needs" and the "wants," and it leads you to achievement. I'm sure that during the reading of this book, you either thought or will think that you could never give up on some things. Because you're so emotionally attached to them and you don't want to lose the beautiful memory that those objects remind you of.

There's a very simple revelation behind this philosophy: memories are formed in your mind and stay in your heart forever. You decide to associate them with objects, and if the purpose is not present, you fear that the memory will fade away. However, fears, like limits, are often just an illusion. The reality is your mind is capable of keeping the memory alive for as long as you choose to. This is the exact reason why people tend to keep so much stuff – it's their treasure full of experiences they hold dear.

If you are still not convinced, we have a minimalist hack for you. If you have an item that has no practical use but holds a treasured memory, try this: Take a picture of the thing, and you can look at it anytime you want without it taking up physical space.

So, if you think you could never give up on TV, your car, your too-many-bedroom home, your closet full of clothes and shoes, your favorite junk food and more – think again. Your mind can adjust to and adopt anything – in this case, the minimalist lifestyle that will bring you a lot more positive changes than your current life does.

What follows are some simple steps, tips, and tricks to build a minimalist mindset:

- Recognize and select your needs. Often, people don't distinguish between what they need and what they want. This is true of material things. For example, we don't need a new appliance – we just want it because we think it'll make our life easier. We don't necessarily need 2-3 cars – we just want them for the same reason. The list goes on How much cabinet, pantry, and counter space all of your instruments occupy? Many machines are not used frequently enough to make life easier. Though a device may initially expedite a cooking task, count the amount of time it takes to clean and reassemble the apparatus after the function.

- Eliminate the "just-in-case" mentality. Much of the clutter in our homes comes from hoarding items that we don't need immediately; rather, we think we might need them in some hypothetical future. We keep those items "just in case" fearing that we won't survive without them. Examples of 'just in case' items to eliminate are all those extra wicker baskets, various craft items. Another way to define 'just in case' items would be non-essential items (Examples: wicker baskets, various crafts, impractical shoes, or stacks of pens you keep). Contrast that with essential items such as fire extinguisher or first aid kits.

Chapter 1: An overview of minimalism

- Take your time. Becoming a minimalist is a massive change, and it doesn't happen overnight. Gradually, you'll start to realize how this lifestyle works and adjusting your expectations should be by the process. For some people, it might happen in a couple of weeks; for some – a month or two and others, it might take longer. Have faith, keep your goals in mind, and everything will fall into place.

- Practice. The beginning may be hard, especially if you haven't tried minimalistic living before. The key to a successful transition is to practice. Start small. Get rid of things you haven't used in years (Especially three years or more); clean the garage; your pantry *etc*. With practice, you'll learn to select objects and classify them as essential or non-essential.

- Make a list of pros and cons. Be honest, objective, and view the question as if it wasn't your own. This can significantly assist in the process.

- Being a new Mindful minimalist will take time and patience. Through this process, you will begin to value people more, objects less, and live life like never before. You will feel freer, as you only let go of all these non-essential items burdening you.

Why simple living is important

As humans, there are essential things we need to survive. We need clothes to keep us warm. We need food to nourish our body. We build homes for shelter.

And then there are things that he wasn't in life, for recreation and consumption.

Today, however, the majority of us want things that didn't exist before. These things could bring joy and satisfaction, or unnecessary obsessiveness and addiction. The Internet has brought us unlimited information about the world around us. If you wanted immediate access to movies, you have Netflix. Instead of collecting music albums, you can download hundreds via iTunes. If you wanted to look smart, a digital bookshelf of literary classics could work its magic for you.

Chapter 1: An overview of minimalism

We can talk to people despite long distances. We can take our work anywhere. You can work on multiple things at once across several screens due to the onslaught of so many apps that could do anything. Life and work become more efficient, fast, and practical.

But progress has its pros and cons. We are bombarded by advertisements that reshape our desire for material possessions. We want bigger houses, faster cars, more advanced technology, fashionable clothes, expensive cuisine, and more.

Consumption is necessary, but in excess, it is not. Many of us work harder for things we may later realize we don't necessarily want. Owning too many things hampers not only our movements but also essential priorities. These priorities a back seat until we understand later that we have lost so much time in pursuing stuff we don't need.

And because of technological advances, we are expected to do more work since everything is almost automated. This leads to the habit of multitasking. It also doesn't help that the current addiction to screens drives most of us to have less sleeping hours, more stress, and unhealthy habits.

Do you feel like you are one of those people mentioned above? Are you working hard but feel like you are not accomplishing much? Do you realize that many of your possessions are stealing too much of your money, time, energy, and focus?

This can all be changed, but you have to change from thinking about decluttering your physical environment and your mind. The first step to achieving this is to have more space to move about and to help clear your head. You need to be in an environment where you are not always stressed out because you have too many things to do, or because you don't have enough time to work on your goals and to be with the people you love.

I believe you will agree with me when I say that the majority of us desire to live comfortably and well-balanced lives. We all want space and enough time to reflect and decide how we want to spend each hour within a day and our future. This necessity for reflection is something that has been lacking in our modern life. We need to pull ourselves back to realize what is important to us.

And all this can be done by applying the concept of Minimalism

Chapter 2:

The Minimalist Mindset

Minimalism appeals to a desire for a simpler life—an uncluttered and unbusy life filled with more meaning, purpose, and joy. This is a healthy desire, and pursuing it can lead to many benefits. Who doesn't want clarity of mind, financial freedom, contentment, a happy home, and better health, just to name a few?

The *Why* of Minimalism

It's important to know why you want to pursue minimalism. Having a firm grip on your *way* to becoming minimalist will be a steady source of fuel for your motivation to be one. This matters as much for those who are just beginning this pursuit as for those who have been after this for a while. And as you experience a minimalist life, you'll likely find new reasons to be minimalist. First, I want to tell you what I mean by *minimalism*.

What exactly is Minimalism?

MINIMALISM IS A TRADE

When I think about minimalism, I don't think about what I must give up. It's not about setting a limit to the number of things I can keep. Instead, it's about what I'm trading. Giving up something is always about trading.

When we shed our excess possessions, we're making room for something better. *Everything has a cost.* When we say yes to one thing, we are saying no to another. A minimalist life is about trading a life filled with clutter, busyness, and noise for a life filled with meaning, connection, and purpose.

MINIMALISM IS LIVING WITH INTENTION

When you apply the philosophy of minimalism to every part of your life, you practice intentionality. You ask yourself questions like: Do I need this? Will this bring me joy? Does this grow my character? When we approach our day with the intention of discovering what brings happiness and contentment, every subsequent action is filtered through this lens of conscious purpose.

MINIMALISM IS AWARENESS

As you apply minimalism and intentionality to your life, you start noticing how the powerful messages of our culture have influenced your past and present decisions.

You may be questioning the value of what you've filled your home with, the work you've chosen, and even the way you connect with other people. Are you spending everything you have in time, energy, and money on possessions, work, and relationships but still longing for more? Go back to less to find more of what you're after.

MINIMALISM IS FREEDOM

Like it or not, we humans tend to make things more complicated than they need to be. We compare our lives to those around us and start thinking we should have what they have, do what they do, and be more like them. Minimalism helps you break free from keeping up with anyone else around you. It enables you to discover what matters more for you and your family. It shifts your focus from what everyone else has, does, or is, to what satisfies you. We are free to focus on what matters when we're less distracted by all the noise and clutter around us.

The Soaring Cost of Excess Stuff

I invite you to think about your stuff for a minute. Think about the things that you own but don't use and may not even like now. Ask yourself if there are some things that you've forgotten that you own. How much time have you spent acquiring and taking care of things? As Henry David Thoreau said, "The price of anything is the amount of life you exchange for it."

We spend a lot of time on our personal belongings. We store them, clean them, find them, repair them, wonder if they're worth fixing, replace them, wonder what model to replace them with, consider what accessories to get with them, and search for the best deal for them. As you can see, personal belongings not only take up physical space but mental energy as well.

Let's face the reality that our deeper, heartfelt desires and goals aren't satisfied by more material goods and a jam-packed calendar. We're probably looking at diminishing returns in this crazy pursuit of *more*—spending our limited resources of time, energy, and money on homes overflowing with stuff and schedules overflowing with commitments, only to be left wanting more. Our overflowing calendars magnify the cost of our favorite material. The busier we are, the less time we have to take care of all of it.

There are tangible costs of our stuff, like money and space, but the higher prices are psychological. In today's culture, material goods have become substitutes for deep and meaningful connections. We strive to acquire possessions and busy calendars, and then ignore the things that give us lasting fulfillment and joy: personal growth, contributing to others, generosity, and healthy relationships.

The actual cost of our excess stuff and chaotic lives reaches far beyond a price tag and a full calendar. Our excessive consumption is killing us and the people we want to be. I encourage you never to underestimate the benefits of removing things you do not need.

Chapter3:

Importance of Minimalism

The less we have on our plate, physically and mentally, the more energy and gratitude we can have for the life we want and the life we have! When people think about the benefits of minimalism, they often think only about the initial interest, such as an uncluttered home. But there are life-changing benefits to gain as you move past the initial purging. It isn't just a simple, clean home we're after. We're trading our excess stuff for things we'll look back on and wish we had more of, like time spent pursuing our passions and purpose and in relationships that bring positive transformation.

Minimalism directs your finite resources of attention, time, energy, and money toward being and doing more of what matters most. With this foundational benefit, you are better able to make the intentional choice to be and do who you're prepared to be and what you're made to do. This benefit is not just for some individuals who have the freedom to make drastic changes in their lives. All of us—including you and your family—will gain from it.

1. Less stress and anxiety

Our excess stuff is most likely affecting the stress levels of our children. The excess visual stimuli are a distraction for them as well. Less to take care of means less to stress about, and this can help us find more clarity of mind. Once the initial dopamine rush of getting something is gone, clutter becomes a constant brain drain. Using MRIs and other diagnostic tools, research has found that confusion hurts our brain's ability to concentrate and process information.

Finding more clarity of mind is possible as we clear away the distractions that come with keeping more than we need and trying to be someone we aren't made to be. Just making a start on this path can give your mind more bandwidth with which to focus on what matters most in your life.

2. Stronger relationships

Humans need to connect with other humans—we don't want to be lonely.

A minimalist home and lifestyle help us put our focus on people, instead of on the stuff they have. There are more energy and space for people and relationships to flourish.

We don't build satisfying connections around possessions—not even shared properties. Links are established around shared experiences. I'm not saying that territories have nothing to do with our relationships. But when we use a lot of our finite time and energy on properties, we're spending time connecting to our stuff and our schedules more than we are relating to other people. Minimalism is making a conscious choice to use things and love people because the opposite will not bring us the connections we long for.

3. Healthy boundaries

Minimalism helps you set healthy boundaries by giving you the clarity to see all the things you're spinning your wheels on. Resetting boundaries to align with priorities is an ongoing process in a minimalist lifestyle, but it's not an unwelcome chore. The rewards of more being and less striving encourage me to keep going on this journey. If I don't prioritize my life, someone or something else will.

4. More time

Keeping more than we need, whether its possessions or activities, brings a fog into our daily lives that make it harder to think clearly. Under the influence of clutter, we may underestimate how much time we're giving to the less critical stuff. Minimalism helps you see how you're spending your time and to think more clearly about how you would like to donate it.

We've found gap time in our family since we began practicing minimalism. This means we aren't living in the land of rushing around between one activity and another. Minimalism has helped us identify the actions, even the perfectly good businesses, which take us away from better things. We no longer feel the pull to participate in every sport and enrichment activity that could benefit our children. Remember, this is a good thing.

5. Less stress about finances

Financial minimalism has given us the freedom to share with those who benefit far more from our excess than we ever will. But we aren't just giving away money or things that we don't need as much as others do. We're giving up money and possessions that we only don't need. Not only do we not need it, but this excess is also at the very least a distraction, and at worst costs us more to keep than to give away!

6. A streamlined home

Imagine having a home filled with no more than what adds value to your life. When you de-clutter, you're more likely to know what you have in your home. Finding what you need when you need it becomes a more manageable task when you develop clutter-free habits. Less frustration means less stress. Like a lot of other people, I strive to live in a clean and uncluttered home but don't want to spend all my free time cleaning it. Having less stuff covering our floors, furniture, and kitchen counters has cut my cleaning time in half. Less time cleaning is more time to do something we enjoy more.

7. Environmental friendly

We waste less when we buy less, and this is good for our planet. For the average American, clothing is cheap and readily available. One result of this is that the average American now generates 82 pounds of textile waste each year. Although I love a deal as much as anyone else, I no longer take pleasure in unnecessary clothing purchases at my local Target.

Minimalism has helped our family take steps toward a zero-waste lifestyle. Just because we still need a weekly garbage pickup doesn't mean we can't or shouldn't keep taking steps to reduce our waste production. When possible, we choose products that can be used for a lifetime. For example, we discarded our plastic water bottles in favor of stainless steel ones. Since we each have and use our water bottle, we keep plastic out of landfills and have fewer dishes to wash every day. Environmental minimalism helps you cultivate earth-friendly decisions, like choosing sustainable and recyclable beauty products, canceling your catalog subscriptions, choosing electronic media for books, magazines, and newspapers, switching to online banking and digital record keeping, carpooling or using mass transit, and limiting your shower time.

A minimalist home produces less waste, which is good for our planet and all of us living on it.

8. Deeper spiritual life

Many of us make a journey of faith to discover what we truly need and who we are meant to be. A spiritual journey can be interrupted by having too much and by having too little. Minimalism nurtures growth and discovery of who we are expected to be. Busyness is likely to give us a false sense of purpose and materialism is expected to provide us with a false sense of being blessed. We might not call it materialism when we post our pictures and stories with the hashtag #blessed on Facebook, Twitter, or Instagram—we probably want to express our gratitude and highlight our moments of happiness. But we can show our appreciation and contentment by giving what we don't need to someone who does need it. We can pursue and share our real purpose when we say no to commitments that don't serve it.

9. Freedom

Ultimately, minimalism gives you freedom. Freedom from consumerism, debt, and anxiety about caring for your possessions. Freedom from the weight of sentimental items. Freedom from guilt to keep things that no longer serve your purpose. Freedom from holding on to your fantasy-self and from measuring up to unrealistic expectations. Freedom to relax and think about what you want to think about. Freedom to say no to additional obligations and to make better connections with family, friends, and neighbors. This is what minimalism is genuinely about.

Chapter 4:

How to Live a Simple Minimalist Life

Most people think that they can accumulate a lot of possessions and still be able to live the dreams that they have. But the problem is that this is not true. Things only get in the manner of being able to live a life where you are free to do what you want and free to do as you please. You need to understand that if you're going to live a life of freedom, then you are going to have to take the time to look at how the things you own are holding you back. Once you come to this realization, you are going to be able to get rid of the things that are doing just that. Then you are going to be able to spend more time on the things that matter to you.

The first thing that you need to do is look at everything that you own carefully and examine what is required and what is not. You need to see which items are used on a regular basis and which are rarely if ever used. Once you have done this, you are to throw out, donate, or sell all of the items that you do not use and keep all the things that you do use on a regular basis. This is the initial and most crucial step toward you achieving the life you want.

Next up is to make sure that you do not bring any more clutter into your home. This means that you stay away from places where you usually buy things for the sake of it, like a shopping mall. If you need to buy an item and you see that you are going to use it on a regular basis then and only then buy it. However, you will come to see that most of the things that you think were necessities were just impulse buys that would have resulted in more crap entering your home. That's all there is to lead a more simple minimalist life.

Get Focused

Before you ever embark on a new journey, it is important to get focused and clear on what you are doing. You want to know precisely why you are taking on a new adventure or path, and what this lifestyle will mean for you. Getting focused gives you the opportunity to completely understand what your motives and intentions are and why you should stay committed when things get difficult, which they always do at one point or another.

With minimalism, you should understand that the lifestyle is more than just living a life free of physical clutter. It is also about living a life free of mental, emotional, and non-physical clutter. You need to learn to stay focused on what you want and stop dwelling on things that do not serve you and have no purpose in your life. You can do that by getting focused and staying clear on what your goals are.

Initially, getting focused might be extremely simple. There are usually two reasons why someone wants to become a minimalist: either they cannot stand looking around at clutter anymore, or they cannot hold all of the restrictions on their time. Because both of these involve stress and discomfort, people are driven to make a change in their life. However, it can be easy to stop making changes once you reach a place of comfort. Or, you may not want to begin because you realize that any difference will be less comfortable than what you are already doing. After all, we tend to stay in lifestyles that are most comfortable to us.

It is crucial that you learn that staying focused and determined takes effort on a constant basis. The focus is a balancing act that you must work towards regularly. The more you work towards it, the more success you are going to have with it. The following tips are going to help you both with getting focused and clear on your path, and with learning to re-center your focus along the way. You will be guided through a couple of journaling exercises which will give you an excellent opportunity to get clear and provide yourself with something to refer back to when it gets difficult. These activities are essential to your success, so it is a good idea actually to invest the time in completing them.

Decluttering methods

Decluttering is essential to starting a minimalist lifestyle. It might seem a shame to get rid of perfectly good items, but there are several ways to justify decluttering so that you don't feel guilty. You need have no qualms about throwing away things that are worn, stained or no longer useful to anyone. Some of your quality stuff can be passed on to people you know. If a friend has often remarked that he loves a particular figurine, something that's not all that important to you, give it to him so he can enjoy it.

You can also donate items. Goodwill, Salvation Army, and other nonprofits receive donations and accept almost anything. A Habitat for Humanity ReStore will be glad for your discarded household fixtures.

You can always hold a garage sale and make a little bit of money while getting rid of things you do not need; you can get to know the neighbors in the process. You can always give away or throw away anything left over. You will be surprised what people will take when it is free. Some nonprofits will even pick up your unsold items at their thrift stores.

There are multiple methods available to help you declutter. I suggest you try out several and pick what works best for you. Decluttering does take time. Don't assume to get it all done in one day, but do set goals to guide you through the process. I suggest you use a calendar to mark down each stage of your decluttering and assign them specific target completion dates.

It's easiest to tackle the process one room at a time. Be aware that cleaning out a closet will usually take most of a day or even two days; it's a big job! Decluttering the kitchen is also a one- to a two-day job.

Some experts say you should do a little decluttering at a time, giving one item away per day or filling one trash bag in a week. Others say it is all or none. They think you should go through every closet and drawer with clothing in it all at one time, so you don't forget what you have.

Remember, you make the rules. If you want to take it slow, take it slow. Just keep in mind that one item a day means it may take your life to complete the decluttering process! However, if you are enthusiastic about becoming a minimalist, get it all done in a week or two and start enjoying your clutter-free lifestyle?

The following are some popular methods of deciding what to discard, with techniques for staying organized during the process:

The 12-12-12 Method

Twelve is a nice round number. It doesn't take long to gather up 36 items and decide what to do with them. To work the 12-12-12 method, you collect things in your house, finding 12 things to put away, 12 things to give away and 12 things to throw away. You can do this once, twice, or three times a week. It's up to you.

The Four Boxes or Baskets Method

Acquire four large boxes that are nearly the same size or go out and purchase four of the same kind of laundry basket. One will be for trash you will throw out, one is for things to give away, one is for things you want to store, and the fourth is for things you want to keep. Take a room and start filling up the boxes or baskets. Once you fill them, get rid of the stuff in the trash box, box up the things you want to give away, then pack and stash what needs to be stored. Take everything out of the fourth plate and ask yourself, "Do I need this? Does it bring me joy?" If the response is yes, then put it in its proper place; otherwise, put it in one of the other boxes.

The Mapping and Rating Method

In this method, you make a map of all the rooms in your house. Mark where the doors and windows are located and draw in the closets. Draw where the furniture sets. Rate each place as to how cluttered it is, marking one for uncluttered, two for somewhat cluttered, three for very cluttered, and four for the last cluttered space. Start with the most cluttered room first and take that map with you.

Mark with an "X" the most cluttered area and start cleaning out there. You can use your 12-12-12 technique or the four-box method in conjunction with this plan.

Acquire Financial Freedom.

I know that many people argue that money is not everything or money is the root of all the evil... etc... But well, this is not true. According to several studies and research work on wealthy people from all around the world, it is now proven that if you are financially free, then you are happier than those people in your age/income group who are not economically free.

Of course, Money cannot buy happiness. But still, up to a certain level of joy, Financial Security is essential. Most of the people are scared of being broke or even bankrupt after their retirement or even before that because of the substantial debt.

In China, most of the people worry about their debt while sleeping at night rather than heart disease and diabetes. This is the scenario of people from everywhere around the world. But people that are Financially Free are not worried about these kinds of financial uncertainties, and that's why they are happier than others in the same age/income group.

Financially free doesn't mean that you should be a millionaire or multi-millionaire. It says that your monthly Passive Income from your various Investments such as Stocks, Bonds, Gold, Real Estate & Businesses or even salary is much more than your monthly expenses. Thus, also suppose if you stop working today, you can live for the rest of your life on the Income you generate from your Investments.

To obtain financial freedom, you must master your inner thoughts and spoken words. Your innermost thoughts are the start of everything that you create. What you focus on expands. Fear-based feelings will manifest themselves into reality if you allow them to grow in your mind. You should concentrate on the things that you want so that it expands and demonstrates in your life. Your words are also crucial as negative words such as "I can't afford it" or "I will never be rich" will send out the wrong message. The universe only responds to thoughts and words of abundance. Other things like creating a spending plan, setting financial goals, learning to invest or even simplifying your life all stem from this simple idea of mastering your inner thoughts.

A word about financial worries

Many people worry about money, how to pay the bills each month. Consumer credit agencies and credit card companies have made it all too easy to run up staggering amounts of debt, offering consumers large credit lines with enticingly low monthly payments.

Many don't realize that the exorbitant interest rates that can come with such credit can put them in a deep hole financially, causing daily worry and stress.

Chapter 4: How to Live a Simple Minimalist Life

One solution: You can cut up your credit cards, close your accounts, and make a three-to-five year plan to get out of debt by living on a budget, within your means, and paying off each credit card bill, starting with the highest interest one first.

Sure, it will take time. But if you're focused on the goal of being debt-free, you can do it, and, often, just knowing you've stopped running up bills and embarked on a plan to get out of debt and build up a savings account instead can make you sleep better at night.

If you feel overwhelmed and you are past due to everything, and bill collectors are calling every night, there's still hope. Contact the folks at Consumer Credit Counseling. There's a branch in almost every medium to large city, and they will help create a recovery plan for you.

Then, they'll contact each credit agency and negotiate a payoff plan for you. If you're in a small town, you can sometimes pay an attorney to settle the payouts for you, anything to stop the interest rates from continuing to bury you under a mountain of debt.

Just remember that no matter what your current situation is, you still have a choice in how you will respond to it. And bear in mind that your present condition need not extend forever. Getting depressed is not the answer. Taking proactive steps to solvency is, and the moment you do, you will feel a massive weight lifted off your shoulders.

That's what making a new plan is for relieving the current stress and looking forward to a modern day. Choose leniency and personal forgiveness toward your past behavior, coupled with a firm resolve not to keep making the same mistakes over and over.

Enough counsel about addressing financial wrongs. Personal finance is only one of many issues or circumstances that may be clouding your mind and keeping you from happiness.

Adopt a Unique Spiritual Outlook

I believe firmly that we all have the power within us to achieve peace. All we have to do is learn to live in the Now. This is a state I try to attain regularly, with limited and tantalizing success.

Chapter 4: How to Live a Simple Minimalist Life

You can, too, by practicing the precepts outlined below.

In this section, I will try to sum up the book's teachings, in the hope that you will find Tolle's precepts enlightening. Tolle encourages us to "observe the thinker" inside all of us. By doing so, we can willfully still the many voices going on in our minds at all times. He does not mean that because we all have an inner dialogue going on inside our heads most of the time that we are crazy or schizophrenic.

He merely means that we can learn to calm that inner dialogue and achieve inner peace, something I believe most of us wish to do at one time or another. He says that experiencing the joy of Being does not come at the expense of clear thought or an awareness of the things around us. Preferably, the state of Being is one of hyper-awareness of our surroundings, a sense of being fully present at the moment. "And yet, this is not a selfish state, but a selfless state. It takes you beyond what you previously thought of as 'your self.' That presence is mostly you and, at the same time, inconceivably more significant than you."

Tolle says that 80-90 percent of most people's thinking is not only repetitive and useless, but because of its dysfunctional and harmful nature, much of it is also detrimental. "Observe your thoughts, and you will find this to be true. It causes a serious leakage of vital energy."

He says that the more significant part of human pain is unnecessary. "It is self- created as long as the unobserved mind runs your life." Tolle stipulates that if you no longer want to create pain for yourself and others, then you must realize that the present moment is all you have. He adds that we should always say "yes" to the Now.

This bears out what we said earlier about living not just one day at a time, but one hour, or one moment at a time, avoiding the possible cares and dangers of the future, and not dwelling on painful happenings or relationships in the past.

Minimalism by lowering your expectations

I once had a friend who told me something wise, "Lower your stress by lowering your expectations."

At the time, I had evolved into something of a perfectionist. I had moved into middle management and expected excellence from myself and those who worked for me. I may have been, looking back on it, something of a pain in the neck to those around me.

I also had developed a fair amount of stress, trying to control many factors that were beyond my control. I didn't want to "lower my expectations." To me, that was tantamount to accepting poor performance in myself and others. Eventually, I got older, and I began to understand the wisdom underlying this concept.

The case for lowering your expectations

In a new study, researchers found that it didn't matter so much whether things were going well. It questioned whether they were going better than expected.

Not that you should walk around gloomy all the time. Having expectations at all, say for lunch with a friend, can lift your spirits as soon as you've made plans.

Take action! This week, reset an expectation. What is a more realistic and enjoyable goal?

Then, refocus on the journey rather than on the destination. What mountains can you climb that you will genuinely enjoy climbing (figuratively speaking), whether or not you ever make it to the top? How can you focus on the present moment, whatever you are doing right now, rather than setting big goals and expectations for the future?

In personal relationships, having realistic expectations will allow you to accept the flaws in others. We need to take responsibility for our lives before we can expect others to do the same.

One of the most significant challenges we face in life is learning to accept people for who they indeed are. Once you realize that your expectations cannot change people, the better off you will be.

Someone else I once heard of had a great way of summing this philosophy up: "Give without expectation, accept without reservation, and love without hesitation." It's all about perspective

Lower your expectations if you want to be fulfilled. Raise them if you're going to make things more efficient.

You can start an exercise regimen to feel better about yourself and achieve contentment. You can also contact well about yourself by taking even a few small steps to improve your self-image. This will give you renewed confidence and boost your self-esteem.

But you must be realistic about the goals you set or the exercise will be one that ends in futility. You must understand your goals clearly and map out the steps necessary to reach them.

Finally, one counselor I read about says her clients are stressed, and then they're stressed about being stressed. Well, meaning people tell them to "get more sleep or exercise" or "start a meditation regimen."

Again, does this sound familiar?

This counselor even says that having some degree of stress is standard, as long as your coping skills can deal with it. That's funny. People who can cope successfully with stress have no need of self-help books on ways to reduce stress. I have often marveled at such people, who must have a hereditary or prominent gene that allows them to slough off the weight that would kill us mere mortals.

Look within yourself

Amanda Christian, writing in the blog tinybuddha.com, says many of us want things because of the way we think they will make us feel. You may wish to a skinnier body because you think it will make you feel happy and loved. You may want a successful career because you think you will feel fulfilled. You want a relationship because you think it will relieve your loneliness.

These things can distract us from looking within ourselves for answers. When they fail to do what we want, we feel disappointed and angry. To release this cycle of disappointment, we need to release the belief that they will save us.

Relax more, judge yourself less

Christian says she learned that the loving voice within, also known as our inner guide, has a bigger plan for us than we have for ourselves. "As it turns out, right now you are exactly where you need to be," she says. The only thing you need to do, Christian adds, to follow the path of your inner guidance is listen to it by releasing your judgments about what you think is happening. You don't have to have everything figured out right now. "Get quiet and listen for guidance about what to do at this moment. Any advice coming from love will be something you can do now. The thought of doing it will make you feel lighter and excited."

Change your thoughts

The first thing I do when I feel any disturbance to my peace of mind is say to myself, 'I am determined to see this person/situation differently.' This is how you step into your power. Everything happens to you, not to you.

You'll be amazed at the shifts in perception that occur when you become willing to release fear and see love instead.

Minimizing Your Home

When you are busy, you do not have a lot of time to devote to getting your home organized. It is then easy for it to get messy, and for the mess to get out of control. It can be challenging to understand where to begin, so to help get you started, here are five quick tips to declutter your home -

1. Do not put off until tomorrow what you can do today.

Procrastination does not make it go away. In fact, it only gets worse and causes you more stress in the long run. Once you had bit the bullet and got on to it, you will feel so much better. Nothing beats looking at a room that is as neat as a pin and looking very attractive. The best part of it is that you have the satisfaction of a job well done.

2. Decide when you will start and how long you will work for before you start. Then stick with it.

Be realistic and make your goal achievable. As you complete the first session successfully this gives you the impetus to get started on your next meeting. Begin by planning what you want to achieve and how, and you can save yourself a lot of time. By setting a time limit for each session, you will still have energy left for the other things you need or want to do.

3. Donate items that you no longer want or need.

If you have some belongings that are still in good order, consider giving them to charity and free up the space they took just lying around, collecting dust. The good thing here is that you do not need to spend any more time maintaining and taking care of them, which gives you more time for other things. It is easy to hoard stuff, in case it comes in handy one day, but let's face it if it is not being used it can't be needed. The other advantage is that most charities are happy to take your donations, and they can be tax deductible as well!

4. Do not spread clutter from one room to another.

It can be straightforward to pick up an armful of clothes and take them down to the bedroom, dump them on a chair and, leave them there! Stuffing all your shoes into your closet or putting a pile of paperwork on a shelf to 'clear' the table is only moving one mess from one place to another. This can make things worse, not better or tidier! You are still not creating any free space and, you will even need to sort those piles out at some point in time.

5. Decide to handle each item once.

Allow yourself enough time to work through one problem area at a time. When looking at the things you are sorting decide where it is going and then put it in its place. The lesser ways you handle an item, the faster you get through decluttering your house. Sometimes it is not possible to touch something only once, but minimize as much as possible how many times you pick up any one thing. As you find a place for each item, it then is more comfortable to keep things tidy, because each element can be put back in its place after use. This has the added advantage of then being able to find those items when needed, saving lots of looking time.

So there you have it - 5 quick tips to declutter your home. They can help you get started quickly and make good progress, but to keep your place decluttered, work on developing it into a habit.

Chapter 5:

Minimalism and happiness

1. Lessen Your Dependencies

We all have our crutches to lean on, unfortunately for lots of us we become dependent on one or more of them. By far the most apparent crutch in our society is alcohol. It is deemed acceptable to become intoxicated or drunk primarily by the younger crowd, and the most common reasoning for the behavior is because 'it feels better to be drunk than not.' That is just an example, and the crutch could be anything, drugs, painkillers, and coffee to name a couple, usually some substance. If you are experiencing hard times and you find yourself turning towards something such as alcohol then refrain from doing so, you will only become dependent on it to get you through hard times rather then relying on yourself. Dependencies create weakness, the more you lessen your dependencies, the more you can strengthen your mind which will allow you take on larger and larger obstacles calmly and without breaking down or losing control of yourself. Which in turn leads to greater control, confidence and of course happiness.

2. Listen to Some Post-Rock

This is related to both relaxing and writing a journal as it achieves similar things. The key is to listen to soothing yet complex music, classical, acoustic, ballads anything goes here but Post-Rock is perfect. Some bands to check out for this purpose are Mogwai, Explosions in the Sky; This Will Destroy You and Russian Circles. Now why do this you ask, it's simple, most of the music people listen to is high energy or tightly focused on a subject of interest. This sort of music is naturally relaxing, and your interpretation creates the subject, it can excite your imagination, emotion and your thoughts. Similar in a way to writing a journal in that your thoughts can lead you places you didn't think they would go, similar to relaxing because, well, it's relaxing. So just throw on a track or two and sit back or lay down, just let yourself go, you may find your mind refreshed afterward. I've also heard it can help soothe people to sleep. If there is anything music can't do, let me know, it can create some happiness.

3. Meditate

This is a prevalent way to decrease stress and increase happiness. If you are not doing it already, then you should start now. Every waking moment we are bombarded with external stimulus whether we notice or not, and our brains must sort through it all at near-instant speed. What meditation does is try to minimize all the stimulus to your brain, create focus, and give your brain some 'me' time. Now you might be thinking that that is what sleep is for but not entirely. When we sleep our body re-energizes itself, and our brain churns through all the information from our day, organizing it, deciding what is essential and what is not so although we wake up fresh and may not know it our brain has been working the entire time. Meditating is easy, only lay down with your hands by your side or sit in a comfortable position then close your eyes and try to blank your mind, you can either focus on only your slow rhythmic breathing or repeat a single phrase or word over and over that is personally significant to you. Do this for about 15 minutes, and you will come out feeling refreshed and better than before, done daily meditation can work wonders for you and of course increase your happiness.

So there you have it, another three good ways to increase your level of happiness. Try not to rely on your crutches so much, listen to some nifty music like Post-Rock and meditate daily. Just remember that as with everything don't go overboard, like going cold turkey on your crutch, neglecting to listen to your usual music or building a meditation annex onto your house.

Chapter 6:

Minimizing your life for peace of mind

Just breathe - So my most significant discovery in my so-called "quest for peace" was how powerful, simple breathing could be. If you feel overwhelmed with the world, just breathe. It will release all of your stress and tensions. If you have forgotten why you wake up every morning and why you try so hard, just breathe. It will put your mind back into focus. If you feel like you can't stop worrying, just blow. It will calm you and stop the worrying entirely. Radically, breathing eases the body while also bringing your mind to the present. So next time any negative feeling(s) overcome you, just breathe.

Chapter 6: Minimizing your life for peace of mind

Purge all of the clutter- Look around you right now. How much clutter is there? Confusion gives your mind the feeling of oppression, Going a little deeper. Why do we have trouble in the first place? Fundamentally, the confusion stems from our inability to let go of the past. It comes from emotional attachments to objects that have significance to us. Living in the past is unhealthy. Start off by putting a lot of them away and work from there. An open workspace with limited clutter does wonders for your creativity and peace of mind.

Find time for yourself- Artist's masterpieces are usually done in solitude, philosophers were often known to venture alone into the woods for extended periods of time, although time with loved ones is a precious gift of life. I believe time alone is almost as valuable. Alone time allows you to organize and unwind your thoughts. It will enable you to find yourself and to become at peace with the self you found.

Find time to disconnect- I love technology, but it's undeniable that it does a toll on your peace of mind. So to put it just, when you're feeling even the least bit overwhelmed, turn off the TV and read a book. You can also turn off your internet and go for a walk or as I mentioned earlier, just breathe.

While this may sound like a highly rational new way of thinking, in my opinion, it is the devolution of the old 20th-century mindset. Our collective society cries out, "Buy! Keep! Collect! What if it becomes valuable? What if you need it? What if Aunt Petunia comes over and asks what happened to the honey jar she gave you from her garage sale pile?" There is so much societal association between possessions and happiness that we cling to the things in our lives that merely drain us of our desire to do...well...anything!

Compulsion to Clutter

I have a good friend who has a shopping compulsion. This particular friend has boxes and boxes of makeup she never uses, piles and piles of clothes she has purchased but never worn, drawers stuffed full of lotions she has used once or twice, but never used up.

What is it about having things that make us feel secure, even to the point that we will refuse to get rid of a broken appliance or keep boxes of old pens and pencils that we never use? Why do magazines like Real Simple sell millions of copies annually by filling their pages with ideas on organization and tidiness, rather than tips on how to stop buying?

We keep items out of insecurity, fear, and, sometimes, genuine happiness. We buy and keep things that we think will make us happy. Whether it is just one more type of blush, medicine that expired five years ago, or another wooden snowman, each of those items, when we put it in the cabinet or on the shelf, symbolizes the happiness we are trying to achieve in our lives. But do they bring joy, all these things?

Nothing More than Feelings

The truth is one you probably already know, but have heard so many times that it has lost its power to impress you. The fact that money cannot buy happiness, that things cannot make you feel secure. There are no words new enough, is no turn of phrase witty sufficient to make it a unique concept all over again.

Or is there?

Chapter 6: Minimizing your life for peace of mind

Look around your home. When you do, does a feeling of accomplishment, an air of tidiness dominate? Do you feel like you have the things you want and there is nothing out of place, no item that you are keeping "just in case?" If so, feel free to skip this chapter and move right on to another one of interest.

But if you are perusing this book, probabilities are there is something about your environment that makes you feel uneasy, unable to relax, or downright suffocated. You may dream of having the ability actually to have a clean home with a minimum of effort. You have probably heard of the half-hour clean-up, but believe it is a mythical beast like a unicorn or Griffin. If that is the case, consider viewing each of your possessions on an individual basis in light of this attitude:

Does this item add peace and happiness to my life, or does it create a feeling of unease?

This may sound like a bizarre mystical kind of idea, but the truth is, everything you have does create either a positive or negative feeling inside of you when you look at it, use it, wear it, sit on it, or touch it.

Chapter 6: Minimizing your life for peace of mind

This is not a statement of an enlightened mind, but merely an observation. Whether your taste runs toward the minimalist bent or the profoundly eclectic, something about each item around you sparks an emotional response. You may have to create a little more difficult about some issues than others to determine which feeling they arose, but ultimately, you like or dislike every individual piece in your home.

How relaxed you feel in your surroundings is directly related to the number of things in your environment that you like or dislike.

I want to take a moment to put my foot down hard on the brakes and add a disclaimer: That does not mean that the only way you can feel relaxed is to spend thousands of dollars to create an ideal environment.

Chapter 7:

Possession and minimalism

To achieve more freedom and more pleasure you will need to try to maintain minimalist principles, i.e., omitting needless things, identify the essential, making everything count, etc. To achieve extreme minimalism, you will learn many things about being minimalist and try to maintain the things which you should follow such as to start by realizing you already have enough, cutting back on clutter, slowly edit everything and possessions and simplifying your schedule.

Minimalism is just a fancy word for keeping your life simple and setting your priorities straight. Being minimalist is a way to achieve balance in your life. By limiting yourself in life to what is essential to my existence, you will have more time for yourself. You will have more time to exercise and cook nice dinners again. You will be able to focus on career goals that matter and not only cranking out the next widget.

The path to a minimalist life is not an easy one. To achieve extreme minimalism my home will be:

a. Less stressful

b. More appealing.

c. Easier to clean.

d. Minimal furniture.

e. Clear surfaces.

f. Quality over quantity.

The description of a minimalist office will be varied for every individual. The most last minimalist post, I imagine, would be to possess no papers or desk or computer or anything of the sort- only yourself. You would believe an utter and maybe lie on the floor.

With extreme minimalism, finances don't have to be one of the most complicated things in your life. To save money, I follow some things that I use cash not credit. I always try not to buy anything unless I need it, and only if I have the money. I think the first best step secret to happiness you can take to be content, right here, right now, is to quit purchasing useless physical things that you consider them to make you happy and the second best step you can take is to start eliminating the clutter in your life. Do this until you've pared down your possessions to the absolute necessities of your life.

Chapter 8:

30 Days to Simplify Your Life

Day 1: Declutter your online life (and stay offline for a day). Just imagine the free time to think more creatively, do productive things, or to spend it with the people you love!

Day 2: Make a list of 3-6 focused goals and priorities for the year.

Day 3: Observe and analyze your daily habits. Are they right for you? Are they productive?

Day 4: Clean the closet. Find inspiration in the Minimalist Wardrobe part of the book.

Day 5: Clean the junk drawers in the house.

Day 6: Limit or entirely give up the TV for a day. Again, minimalism is about gaining back your time wealth which is our only non-renewable resource. Recommended reading on time wealth is 'Rich Dad, Poor Dad.'

Day 7: Recycle whatever can be recycled or throw away that random item (s) that you can't remember its function. (Examples: random chargers, cords, etc.)

Day 8: Pick a corner or two in the house and remove at least one item that doesn't belong there. The more, the better, but start with 1-3.

Day 9: Gather your kids and clean the toy chest together.

Day 10: Get rid (or donate) or sell (eBay, Craigslist, etc.) 2 of the "just in case" items.

Day 11: Toss at least 15-20 items you don't like, need, use or keep "just in case." Use the 24-month rule. If you haven't used or even picked up an item in 24 months chances are they are "just in case" items.

Day 12: Start the day with meditation. Keep your TV, computer, internet, and other electronic devices turned off until lunch, even at work if you can help it.

Day 13: Clean the kitchen. Raid the pantry cabinet and toss everything you haven't used more than 2-3 months such as unhealthy, refined, sugary, fatty foods, *etc*. Refer to the Minimalist Home part of the book for tips and tricks. (We recommend the "4-Hour Body" for help in eating habits and overall health and exercise hacks.)

Day 14: Place your shoes in one place and think carefully about them. If there are pairs, you haven't worn more than once, either donate them or give them away. You can always find useful advice in the Minimalist Wardrobe section of the book for help.

Day 15: Items with sentimental value. If you're not ready to live without these items, consider making something of them. Create a DIY project for them and put them together as one.

Day 16: Wear absolutely no make-up for the day. If your profession doesn't allow this, choose one of your days off and keep a clean face. You'll instantly feel the difference and lightness on your skin.

Day 17: Today, commit to not buying anything for 24 hours straight. No exceptions to this rule.

Day 18: Clean the bathroom thoroughly. This also means going through the drawers and cabinets and getting rid of everything that you don't use, need, or doesn't belong in the bathroom.

Day 19: Create a simple morning ritual that you can stick to. (Aim for 5 minutes of meditation, exercise, reading, etc.)

Day 20: Analyze the last five purchases. See if these items were something you needed or just something that you bought on sale or because you liked them.

Day 21: Downsize on your commitments. Face the fact that they take up a lot of your valuable time and that you'd be better off without them. It's hard to say no to friends and close ones, but eventually, they'll move on, and you'll feel liberated.

Day 22: Organize a happy day. Today, you're not allowed to complain – just to be grateful. Write down the things that bring you the most happiness and be thankful for them. Forget about the things you don't have. It's one of the leading principles of a mindful minimalist (but it's also authoritative life advice) – to be happy here and now.

Day 23: We've all been multitaskers at one point. Today, try to take tasks one at a time. Hard if you're used to the rush of getting things done as soon as possible. But today, take it slow and dedicate your full attention to one thing at a time.

Day 24: Make your bedroom heaven-like. It should be the calmest and most relaxed room in the house according to Feng Shui, so take the time to make your bedroom a place where you can unwind and enjoy yourself. There shouldn't be electronic devices or a TV in the bedroom. A simple bed, nightstands, lamps, and a closet are excellent. You can have a small library if you want to read before bed but keep the décor simple. All flat surfaces should contain 2-3 pieces of décor or pictures with frames. The walls should be clean, in a soft color and if possible, with no views. Keep one alarm clock in the bedroom and get rid of the rest.

Day 25: Do the laundry without thinking about it being a dull, boring activity. The task is not to just do the laundry, but to accept its nature. Don't think of it as an arduous task. Just grab the basket, load the machine and leave. That's it.

Day 26: Go for a nice, relaxing walk. How many times have you taken intentional strides rather than walking (rushing) to the store? Very few, I know. So, today, ask your loved ones to join you for a pleasant walk around your neighborhood.

Day 27: Take a look at your finances. Is there anything in the past month that you bought but shouldn't have?

Day 28: Use your day off to relax, spend time with your family, have some fun or indulge in your hobbies. Don't work on your day off. (No e-mail peaks, answering a quick call, etc.)

Day 29: Go out and have fun. Go somewhere new, where you don't need to spend tons of money to have a good time. Go to a park, play mini-golf, or meet a friend for coffee.

Day 30: Remember and briefly journal about the past 30 days. It's not going to be perfect, but it's a pretty good start. Note: if you had any problems sticking to the plan or think there's a particular area to improve, you could always upgrade it the next time.

Chapter 9:

Tips and tricks to minimalism

1. Write down your Reasons

The very first step to getting clear is knowing precisely what your reasons are for becoming a minimalist. You need to understand what is compelling you to make the change, and why you are so dedicated. It is essential that you are completely clear on why you are making these changes and that the reasons are important to you. When we are passionate about our purpose, we are much more likely to succeed in what we set out to accomplish.

While you are getting clear on your reasons, take out a piece of paper and write them down. Some people may benefit from merely writing this down on a page in their journal, whereas others may want to take some time with it and turn their reasons into a piece of art that they can keep in a highly visible spot each day. What you choose to do will be up to you, but the most important thing is that you have your reasons readily available.

When you embark on a new journey in life, it can be easy to have mental "relapses" which will draw you back into a previous way of thinking. You may fall back into old habits or patterns and think "well, just this once!" But it's that exact mindset that leads you towards having a cluttered environment. It is during times like this that you want to go back to your written list of reasons and feel into them. Feel the emotion you put behind them and let it rise to the surface for you. The more you can genuinely feel those emotions, the easier it will be for you to remember why you are a minimalist and stay true to your desires.

2. Reclaim Your Time

So much time is wasted when you are trapped in a lifestyle that is solely focused on acquiring the latest and greatest. You spend several hours working, often at a job you don't even like. This generates stress, grief, anger, frustration, and other unwanted emotions that you must face on a regular basis. Then, you must spend time maintaining all of the objects you have acquired. You need to organize them, reorganize them, clean them, service them, and otherwise preserve them. Then, you need to find the time to use them, which you likely rarely ever do spot, so you often end up acquiring objects that merely sit around for you to look at. If you travel or go anywhere, you likely bring more than is required just because you are too guilty to leave something behind knowing that you spent your precious money on it, which is a direct symbol for a time in your subconscious and potentially even in your conscious mind. Then, of course, you must invest time in acquiring more. So, you spend several hours in stores and malls getting frustrated over lineups, other shoppers, and anything else that may upset you. You may go into debt to acquire new things, or you may merely scrape from paycheck to paycheck because you don't want to stop purchasing new belongings. It can be a complicated trap to get stuck in.

Chapter 9: Tips and tricks to minimalism

Being a minimalist means that you get to reclaim your time. You get to stop working so hard to earn money to pay for items you don't have time to use, much less appropriately maintain. You get to stay spending hours a day working to pay off debt, cleaning, and staring at your house full of unused objects. You had the opportunity to thoroughly free yourself from all of the burdens that come along with these actions, both emotionally and physically. Ultimately, you get to reclaim your time to live a life that you want. You can do anything you want with the time that you retrieve; the choice is entirely up to you.

In the beginning, it is a great idea to take a page from your journal and write down all of the things you wish you had time for. What do you want to do that you haven't done because you don't have time? What are the things that you have been putting off because there never seems to be a spare moment for you to complete them? How are you suffering in your own life because you don't give yourself enough time to enjoy it? This list is something you should refer to on a regular basis. As you adopt the minimalist lifestyle, you will want to start checking things off of this list. If you ever feel unsure of what to do or where to go next, use this list as an opportunity to guide you. You can even build on the record as new ideas come up, regardless of how far or deep into your minimalist journey.

The most considerable part of being a minimalist is all of the free time you have. Many minimalists are even able to reduce their hours and go down to working part time instead of full time because they only don't need all of the extra money and they would rather spend time enjoying their life. Many even get to quit their job altogether and pursue a career that they are passionate about because they are no longer fearful of what will happen if they don't have a job to return to should anything go wrong. The freedom that you gain from minimalism is unparalleled, and it is something you can look forward to enjoying your minimalist journey.

3. What Do You Value?

A significant part of the minimalist journey is learning about what you value most. When you are clear on what matters most to you, then you know exactly how to spend your time and resources on creating a life that you love, which is what minimalism is all about. You should spend some time getting to know what you value and becoming clear on it.

A great way to do this is to take your journal and start journaling. Write down what matters most to you, and what you want to gain from life. What experiences make you feel productive with joy and happiness? What makes you excited to wake up and experience each new day as it comes? These are the things you want to enrich your life with. You should give yourself the opportunity to experience these as often as possible. When you are a minimalist, you have less to worry about in regards to taking care of your belongings and gaining more. Instead, you have the gift of more free time, which means that you get to spend your free time however you want.

The other reason why it is essential to know what you value is that it allows you to decide what you want to purchase and own in life. For example, if you appreciate the ability to hop in the car and go anywhere then you may want to keep your car, whereas if you don't mind taking public transit, it may be more beneficial if you get rid of your vehicle. The same goes for virtually anything else you may own.

4. Saying "No"

Learning to say "no" is essential, and it should be one of the first things you learn as a minimalist. You need to know how to say no to bringing more belongings into your house, how to say no to keep belongings in your home, and how to say no to doing things you don't want to do.

Many people believe minimalism is all about items, but it's not. It's about your time and your lifestyle as well. It is about eliminating anything that does not serve your highest good and learning to say no to anything that does not bring you joy. You want to learn how to say no and mean it, and never waiver in your answer. There is never a good enough reason to do something that does not make you feel good overall.

Saying "no" can be hard at first, especially if you are not used to doing it. The more you practice, however, the easier it will be. You should learn to say no to smaller things first: shopping, bringing jobs home, joining e-mail newsletters, and other more accessible things. As you get used to it and it becomes easier for you, you can start saying it to

5. Minimalism is a Journey

Minimalism is a journey, not a long goal. You are not going to wake up one morning with a trophy on your shelf because you 'accomplished' minimalism. Instead, minimalism is a lifestyle. You are going to be working towards your minimalist lifestyle for the rest of your life, or until you no longer desire to be a minimalist. But fear not, if you aren't already in love with it most people find that they do become passionate about minimalism and therefore it becomes easier to maintain the journey as they go on.

Any good lifestyle is a journey. As such, you can expect that your minimalism path will have ups and downs, the ins and outs, twists and turns and all sorts of unexpected events. Nothing will go as planned, and in most instances, that is the beauty of life itself. These are just some of the things that you can look forward to enjoying during your minimalist journey.

Knowing that minimalism is a journey is very important. It means that you are not going to go into it thinking that you will master it or that it will all become more comfortable overnight. While it is comprised of many skills, it is not something that you can just learn and then walk away from. The balance that is required to maintain a minimalist lifestyle takes constant maintenance to ensure that you are not depriving yourself of your basic needs, nor that you are overindulging in things that you do not need. You will always have to maintain this balance using tact, mindfulness, and practice. But, as with any pleasant journey, it is entirely worthwhile if you stay committed to the process.

Minimalism is a beautiful opportunity to learn about yourself and the things you love. You gain the ability to become the person you desire to be, and you can have any experience you want in life. The first part of mastering your mindfulness journey and your skills is to realize that you will never thoroughly learn them. Then, you need to get focused and find ways to stay focused on purpose of your journey. Once you have, you will be ready to have any experience you desire in life. The money, time, and resources will be available to you because you have gotten your priorities straight.

6. Store Things Out of Sight

Many people feel compelled to store things on the counter, or in a space where they can grab it and then toss it back down. While this might be convenient for the grabbing it part, it can also be inconvenient for the rest. After all, rolling things back down often leads to mess, and the mess is likely what lead you to minimalism, to begin with. The first thing you need to do is learn to store items properly.

Ideally, you want to store things out of sight. In drawers, cabinets, cupboards, and closets is a great place to keep items that you aren't using every single day. This means that you do not have to look at it, aside from when you want actually to use it. The key is to make sure that when you are organizing things back into these out-of-sight places, that you are still keeping them organized and under control. You do not want to have them cluttering up your out-of-sight areas, as this will merely lead to more stress. Instead, put them away in an organized and logical fashion. This keeps everything out of sight so that your physical surroundings are cleaner, and it remains everything easy to access and use.

7. Reduce Cooking Time

Many people dislike cooking for lengthy periods of time. If you love cooking and don't mind cooking on a regular basis, then this doesn't apply to you! However, if you dislike cooking and often find yourself eating "convenience" items that are costly and take up space, it might be time to learn how to cook without spending so much time doing so!

Meal prepping is a great way to get a bunch of cooking out of the way so that you don't have to worry about cooking so much on a regular basis. You can prepare meals for a few days at a time so that all you have to do is heat them up and eat them! Another great idea is ingredient prepping. This means that you pre-peel, cut, chop, slice, dice, cube, and store items in a way that makes them easy to cook with. That way when it comes time to prepare, you merely grab enough to melt with and begin the cooking process!

8. Delegate

Not everything has to be done by you. It may feel like you have to do everything alone, but the reality is that you do not. You can easily delegate tasks elsewhere so that you have more time to focus on you and what you want to and need to get done. If you have family living with you, this is easy. Only create a chore-list, and everyone has their unique tasks that they are expected to get done to keep the house operating functionally on a daily, weekly, and monthly basis.

If you live alone, on the other hand, it may be a bit harder to delegate. However, there are still tasks that you can transfer out. For example, if you hate grocery shopping you can order groceries right to your door. There are many services available that offer local-delivery of fresh ingredients. In fact, you can even find services that will deliver locally-sourced organic items that are healthy and convenient. You can also delegate other tasks as well, depending on what you are looking to charge. Some people even hire maids or housekeepers with all of their spare money, to keep them from having to do any of the extra work around the house!

9. Take Breaks

Taking regular technology breaks is essential. As a society, we spend an enormous amount of time attached to devices. Our screen time racks up fast, and we often don't even realize it's happening. Between all of our unique tools, it can be easy to lose time in the online space. A great way to reclaim your time is to take regular tech breaks.

Tech breaks mean that you put away all unnecessary technology for a period. You might do daily tech breaks for a few hours per day, 24 hours break once per week, or even longer breaks. Exactly how long you choose to take tech breaks and how often is up to you, but it is recommended that you take them frequently. This gives you an opportunity to recall how to experience joy in life, without having to rely on the instant gratification of technology that often does not serve our highest good.

When it comes to taking tech breaks, you want to eliminate things such as computers, tablets, cell phones, smart watches, televisions and gaming devices. Stuff you need for cooking, fobs to enter your house or your car, and other such technology devices are perfectly acceptable to continue using. The benefit comes from reducing and eliminating screen time on a regular basis so that you can stay focused on life itself and all that life has to offer. These breaks are excellent at helping you eliminate technology addictions and reclaim your time.

10. Clean Up Social Media

We often spend a great deal of time on social media. A good idea is actually to clean up your social media. On a regular basis, you should unfollow pages and groups you don't like, eliminate friends you do not enjoy having around, and clean up your pages so that they are more favorable to you.

Spending a significant amount of time-consuming information on social media means that you are exposing yourself to a volatile environment. However, you do have a degree of control over what you see and who you see online, which means that you have the opportunity to make it a more favorable environment for yourself. You should take time regularly to clean up your social media accounts so that they remain as positive as possible. That way, any time you spend on your social media accounts will be positive and practical.

11. Morning Routines

There are many pieces of information floating around about what makes an effective morning routine, but something to consider is what doesn't make a solid morning routine. Ineffective morning routines are virtually any routine that has too many things going on. In the morning, you likely have two goals: wake up in a positive mood and acquire enough energy to tackle the day ahead of you. Every single activity you do in the morning should fulfill these needs. If you find you are partaking in any morning routine activities that are not beneficial to you, then you should remove these events from your routine. It is not always necessary to replace them with anything else; you merely need to create a morning routine that serves you.

Many times you will read that a routine should be an absolute length or include some aspects to be productive. The reality is that you can have a productive 10-minute morning routine, or you can have a productive 45 minute or more extended morning routine. The amount of time it takes you to complete your routine and what is specifically involved is unique to you, and it should only consist of things that help you feel energized and confident about your day. If it just takes you five minutes to do that, great! If it makes you an hour to do this, that's completely fine as thoroughly.

12. Other Routines

There are many different routines you partake in throughout your day, as well. In many instances, we establish a method and never revisit it to see if we are using the most efficient manner available to us. It is a good idea to visit routine tasks you do on a regular basis to make them more efficient and effective, if possible.

For example, perhaps you always take the same way to work, but due to the installation of new traffic measures, there is a new route that would be quicker or easier for you to choose. However, perhaps because you never revisit your routine, you are still making the long way to work. Now would be an excellent time to visit this method and change it. Alternatively, perhaps you always do the dishes by washing and thoroughly drying and then rewashing them, when in reality you can directly learn to stack them more efficiently so that you do not have to wipe them in between. In this case, you can only stack them better, or wash them more frequently, and make the task significantly more comfortable.

It is a good idea to take a look at anything you do on a daily basis without thinking about it and find any ways you might be able to enhance these routines to become more efficient and efficient. The better these methods serve you, the more relaxed you are going to be able to get through them and spend the rest of your free time enjoying life.

Your time is valuable, and a significant part of minimalism is recognizing the value in your time and spending it wisely. Many people place an enormous amount of money and material objects and fail to realize how negatively this all affects their time, which tends to be more valuable than money or substantial items. Minimalism is all about learning to replace your value on time and spend it in a way that serves you. You want to spend your time in a way that is effective and efficient so that you can gain the most enjoyment and positivity out of life possible.

13. Forget About Perfection

Something vital for you to learn is that you need to forget about perfection. Perfection is something that adds stress to our lives and makes it harder for us to enjoy life itself. We spend so much time trying to get everything right that we fail to spend time doing. Applying minimalist skills to your life means that you eliminate the need to be perfect and you learn how just to be. Of course, it doesn't say that you don't need to give it you're all. Instead, it means that you just give it your best and then you appreciate it.

Forgetting about perfection and focusing on doing means that you accomplish more in your life. When you let go of your attachment towards doing things entirely, you give yourself the freedom to feel more confident and happy with what you do accomplish when you try your best. You take away the constant feelings of inadequacy and incompetence, and you give yourself the opportunity to feel powerful and confident.

14. Do What You Love

You should practice investing time in doing something you love every single day. Waiting to enjoy time doing what you love is never beneficial, and it can reduce your quality of life. Doing something you like every single day gives you the opportunity to enjoy your life every single day, as well. You don't have to do something major, but you should do at least one thing per day to help you enjoy life more.

Some ideas of what you might do include: cooking or eating a meal that you love, going on a scenic walk somewhere you like, practicing a hobby or activity that you enjoy, or doing any other number of smaller things you want. You might also do something more significant, such as travel somewhere, take a new class, or do something more involved that you would want to do. There is no limit to what you can or can't do when you are doing what you love. Instead, only do it.

Also, you should learn to turn everything into something you enjoy more. You may not necessarily love everything, but you can certainly make it more enjoyable for you. For example, instead of just cleaning the dishes see if you can turn it into a game and make it more enjoyable. Or, instead of only sweeping the floors, set the broom into your make-shift microphone and have an at-home concert for one. There are so many ways to turn everyday activities into ones that you love creatively; there is no reason to spend each day doing mundane things out of obligation.

15. Evaluate Your Schedule

Take some time to think about your schedule. Do you enjoy everything that is on it? Is it fulfilling you or making you feel happy? If you are not satisfied with your program, you need to adjust it to make it fit your needs. If it is overwhelming, find a way to tone it down and make more time for relaxation and peace. If your schedule is underwhelming, find some new activities that you can add to your regular schedule. Sometimes you may not have an overwhelming or underwhelming plan but rather very little of what's on it lights you up and makes you feel happy. If this is the case, you should find a way to add more to it that will bring you joy and make you love your life even more.

Your schedule can be a fantastic tool to help you experience more joy, or it can be a dangerous device that destroys your happiness. If you can manage your schedule wisely, you can have an incredible selection of plans set up that allow you to control your responsibilities and enjoy life itself. Ideally, you want to learn how you can balance your schedule in this harmonious way.

16. Explore the World

Exploring the world is a valuable means to add happiness, joy, and education into your daily life. Of course, most of us can't pack up and explore the world every single day or at the drop of a hat. However, living a more minimalistic lifestyle means that you have much more freedom to explore your way. With fewer expenses and more time, you can do whatever you want for the most part. You should take advantage of this by exploring the world.

You can explore the world around you, or you can travel out and explore elsewhere in the world. There is no limit or rules on what you can or should do when you are investigating. Directly go where your heart takes you. Each new exploration will bring you so much value and knowledge in your life, and most will bring about a broad sense of joy and happiness that enrich your life in ways that other learning resources only cannot.

The world is a brilliant place, and one of the joys of being a minimalist is that it becomes easier for you to explore and enjoy the world. Whether you are hiking, camping, flying, traveling by train, going across countries, or staying in your backyard, nothing beats exploring the world around you and getting to know it better.

17. Do Something New

Have you ever felt like time just melts away? One moment it's a blistering hot summer day, and you're sipping an iced drink, and the next moment it's a cold winter day three years later, and you're in the same spot, only drinking a hot beverage? Research suggests that time melts away because we are continually doing the same thing every day. Average individuals wake up, go to work, spend eight hours working, come home, relax, go to bed, and then do it all over again.

As a minimalist, you have the perfect opportunity to break this cycle and lead a life where every day is precious and diverse from the last, and each one is memorable and serves a purpose in allowing you to be a happier version of yourself. All you have to do is practice doing something new each day. Or at the very least, something new each week. You can do something as small as making an original recipe or driving a new route, or something more substantial like traveling to a new place or picking up a new hobby. Doing something new breaks up the mundane and puts some pep back into your routine. It makes each day stand out and unique from the last, and from the rest that is yet to come. It makes life exciting and keeps sparks. Time will slow down a little as each day won't melt into one another, making life difficult for you to enjoy overall. It is indeed an excellent opportunity to retake control over your life and start living one that you love, to the fullest.

18. Release Ties

How many times are you holding onto because you are too scared to let go? Or, because giving go would be too inconvenient. These relations may be to friends, objects, places, or any other number of things that you hold onto in life.

Chapter 9: Tips and tricks to minimalism

Relationships are common, and you will never get rid of your tendency to create relations towards stuff in your life. However, it is essential that you regularly weed your life and rid yourself of the relationship that does not serve you or bring you joy in life.

Releasing ties gives you the opportunity to let go of the past and open yourself up to bigger and better things. You are granted the chance to refresh yourself and open up space in your life. You stop feeling guilty or even ashamed around specific people, places, or things and you start feeling free once again.

It can be hard to release ties, primarily when we have invested a significant amount of time, emotion, or energy into keeping them. However, the value you can gain from freeing yourself from those ties is immeasurable. Think about how much more devastated you will be if you invest even more time, emotion and energy into something that will serve you. Eventually, it is going to filter out, either because it naturally ends or because you just can't take any more. It is better to cut ties when you are in control and have the power to do so on your own.

19. Fall in Love with Yourself

You are the only person you have to live every single day of your life with. Others will come and go. Some will be there for a long time, but none will ever be immediately by your side for every day of every minute of your life. Only you will be. If you don't take the time to fall in love with yourself and create a relationship with yourself that you love, you aren't going to have much fun in life.

Falling in love with yourself is essential, and you should invest in it every day. Think of it like a marriage: if you don't spend the time to work on it, it will fall apart. Of course, there are going to be ups and downs, but you should always take the time to be gentle with yourself and love yourself as you would your spouse. Only, enjoy yourself even more. You are valuable, and you are worth it, and as a result, you should always find the time to fall in love with yourself on a daily basis. You deserve it.

20. Evaluate Your In-Home Entertainment

How much time do you spend entertaining in your home? For many of us, we don't consider on a daily or even a weekly basis. If this is true for you, then you need to take some time sorting through your stuff and eliminating what you don't need. There is no need to hold on to things for entertaining guests if you rarely have guests over. This only requires you to use up storage space for something you don't need, which goes against the fundamental values of minimalism. It is time for you to get honest with yourself about your entertainment schedule and reduce your entertaining items to reflect that program.

Your daily life can be significantly affected by minimalism. We frequently find ourselves living an everyday life that is uncomfortable, unfulfilling, and often filled with unnecessary activities. If you want to make a change in your life, you need to embrace minimalist values beyond just your physical belongings. You need to be willing to apply them elsewhere in life too so that you can free yourself from all that does not serve you or bring you joy and lead a life that does.

Chapter 10:

How to Maintain Your Minimalist Life

Maintaining your minimalist lifestyle is equally as important as adopting it, and it is the harder part of being a minimalist. Eventually it will become more comfortable, but in the beginning, this will be the hardest part.

See, in the very beginning when you are getting rid of everything and seeing "the light at the end of the tunnel" it can be straightforward to truck on as a minimalist. The cathartic effect of seeing clear spaces in your home and your life is so satisfying that you almost get onto a sort of "minimalist high" that feels so good. But then one day you are going to run into an experience where you are going to feel compelled to purchase something you don't need, or you are going to come home and realize that you have brought home several items you didn't need. And you might feel like you are back to square one. This is because the honeymoon phase of the new lifestyle has changed.

This honeymoon phase exists with any new lifestyle. It is often what people refer to when they say "the novelty wore off." But, if you want to be a true minimalist, you need to work past the dropping off of the honeymoon phase and continue working towards being a minimalist. Otherwise, you are going to end up back in the same place you were when you started: either staring at a room full of clutter saying "I can't do this anymore" or staring at a jam-packed schedule that is full of unhappy appointments saying "I can't do this anymore." It will not serve you to go back on what you have created up until this point.

Setbacks are expected, and difficult times are going to happen. Every new lifestyle comes with a point where your honeymoon phase ends and the real settling in begins. When this happens to you depends on you, how excited you were to change your lifestyle, and what the lifestyle change meant to you. However, you should realize that it is going to happen. When it does, you are going to want to be equipped with knowledge on how to handle the setbacks that may occur.

Maintaining your minimalist lifestyle will become difficult for a short period. However, eventually you will push through that time, and it will become easier. Soon enough it will become second nature to you, and you will realize that the value you gain from the lifestyle outweighs the minor inconveniences you may experience in your daily life from time to time. The following tips will help walk you through this maintenance period and teach you how you can make your minimalist lifestyle stay for good.

1. Take a Shopping Hiatus

It is essential to know when to stop shopping. Once you have everything you need, there is rarely a need to acquire more. Such an action would be a consumerism lifestyle, not a minimalist lifestyle. If you want to maintain your minimalism, you need to take regular shopping hiatuses. Only purchase what you need, and refrain from buying anything more. You can even take it one step further and make total breaks every now and again. For example, try not spending money for an entire week, not even on food. Most people can quickly do this by consuming the food that they have built up in their fridge.

Shopping hiatuses remind us to stop spending what we don't need to spend and to instead invest in what matters. Additionally, they teach us to find joy elsewhere in life, such as where money can't buy happiness. There are many things you can do instead of spending money; it merely takes some time to discover what and how. With each shopping hiatus, you will become even better at lasting longer and still having a fulfilling life for the duration of your break. Consider it a minimalist game!

2. Quality over Quantity

When you are shopping, always make sure that you look for quality over quantity. There is no value in having a significant number of things that do not hold any value. Instead, you want to invest in things that will bring value to your life.

Clothing that lasts, cleaning products that work well and furniture that lasts are all the better than having a significant number of items that fall apart or don't do their intended job.

One of the many pitfalls of the consumerism lifestyle is the "I'll just buy it cheap now so that I can buy more items and then I will replace it with something better later." Ever notice how later never comes, and items often get replaced with more cheap items? That is because they shop with this mindset every single time. Instead, go in with the intention of coming out with nothing except the best that will fit exactly what you need. If you need a couch find the one that brings you joy, serves its purpose well, and will last for a long time. That way, you don't see yourself buying another couch in a few months or a year because you invested in one that fell apart fresh off the delivery truck.

3. Ditch Sales

Sales are a high consumerism environment that you need to learn to ditch as a minimalist. Sales encourage us to spend more money than we wanted to and bring home more items than we meant to. They quickly lead to us having a significant amount of clutter overrunning our house once again. As a minimalist, you need to ditch the sales.

The only time you should attend a sale is if you have something concrete you are looking for and you know that it will be on sale and you have the discipline to go in, get that, and leave. If you don't, you should not go. Going in and coming out with more than you needed or wanted is dangerous, as it leads you back to the consumerist lifestyle. It is best to ditch the sales altogether. At the very least, never go into one without a clear goal and plan.

4. Focus On Your Mindset

Your mindset is the most significant player when it comes to succeeding in any lifestyle. When you want to maintain a minimalist lifestyle, you need always to be thinking like a minimalist. Look for ways to reduce the number of harmful attachments and ties you have in your life and ways to enhance the number of positive ones. This will help you feel better about yourself and your life on an ongoing basis. Your mindset is always the most significant player in whether or not you will succeed in what you have set out to accomplish.

Remember how you were encouraged to get clear on why you wanted to be a minimalist in chapter one? Having these written down makes it easy for you to work on your mindset on a regular basis and keep yourself on track with the lifestyle you desire to live. Eventually, it will become second nature, and you won't even have to think twice: you will just be a minimalist by nature. Until then, always stay very focused on your mindset and maintaining it to be a minimalist.

5. Continue Practicing

Minimalism is a journey, as you have already learned. You always have to be willing to continue practicing. There are going to be times where you have a hiccup, and you spend more than you should have, or you bring home more than you intended. You will still experience buyer's remorse and wish you would have spent your money on something different. You live, and you learn, minimalism won't take you away from that rule of life. However, the most significant point is that you keep practicing. The more you practice being a minimalist and staying balanced in your lifestyle, the more success you are going to have. Nothing comes easy, not even if you make it come naturally to you.

6. Find Inspiration

Keeping your ability to stay functional as a minimalist means that you need to learn how you can find inspiration to keep on track with your lifestyle. Inspiration can be found in many places, from social media to magazines and even in the local minimalist community.

Inspiration can come in many forms. You might feel inspired to reduce the amount of stuff you use, encouraged to find new ways to use things you have, and feel encouraged to live life more comfortable. Maybe you will feel inspired to spend your free time in a better way that allows you to enjoy your life. Finding inspiration is an essential way for you to continue being happy, enjoying life, and living as a functional and successful minimalist.

7. Make Minimalist Friends

As a minimalist, it can be hard to spend time with consumers. While you likely don't judge other people for their way of living, it can be challenging to pay life the way you want to spend it. A lot of time consumers do not have enough money to live life the same way that minimalists do. They may also want to spend time shopping and otherwise spend money on things that don't mean as much to you anymore. Spending time with people like that can be hard.

While you don't need to let go of your consumer friends, it can be beneficial to acquire new minimalist friends. You want to find people who live life with the same values as you and who can help you along your minimalist path. Being friends with other minimalists allows you the opportunity to be friends with those who can help you advance along your route, who recognize your values and understand your motives, and who can enjoy life with you in a way that enriches your life.

8. Live Life to the Fullest

One of the biggest reasons why people become a minimalist is so that they can live life to the fullest without the holdbacks of material belongings and the expenses they bring about. You just can't become a minimalist if you aren't going to live your life to the fullest. The best way is to make sure that you are embracing every single day and getting the maximum pleasure out of it that you possibly can. The more you enjoy each day, the more satisfying and fulfilling your lifelong journey is going to be.

Life is about joy, entertainment, satisfaction, growth, learning, exploring, and so much more. It is crucial that you learn to take advantage of these qualities and infuse them into your daily life. The more you enjoy your life, the more you are going to enjoy who you are and feel fulfilled in your life.

As well, people who genuinely enjoy life are less likely to stress shop, and therefore they will be more likely to continue enjoying life to the fullest. It can be easy to feel stressed out and head out to the stores to fix any ailment they are grappling with what is known as "retail therapy."

Chapter 10: How to Maintain Your Minimalist Life

The reality is, however, retail therapy is more damaging than positive. Retail treatment leads to you spending money you didn't intend to, which can lead to you having less pay for what you need and therefore becoming further stressed out. If you want to make a change, you need to learn to stop using retail therapy as your go-to source, which keeping your stress in check. Living life to the fullest can help you do just that.

Maintaining your minimalist lifestyle is not as hard as it may seem. There are many natural ways that you can keep your lifestyle in check without ever feeling as though you are lacking or you have less than others. In fact, the wealthiest people are those who feel genuinely satisfied with what they already have in life. Those who want more will probably never find it through purchasing more and more belongings. The journey inside is the only way to find pure satisfaction and fulfillment, so when you learn to see that, then all of your material possession suddenly lose such a grand meaning in life. It becomes much easier to maintain your lifestyle, and in fact, it becomes so profoundly fulfilling that you will likely never think about living any other way ever again.

Chapter 10: How to Maintain Your Minimalist Life

Remember, minimalism is a journey, and you are going to have ups and downs. You may still find yourself following old habits that you have developed for many years. That is okay and completely normal. Be gentle with yourself, learn from it, and find a way to bring yourself back into the world of minimalism. Eventually, it will become much more accessible to stop impulse shopping before it even begins, allowing you to maintain your minimalist lifestyle effortlessly honestly.

Conclusion

Thank you again for purchasing this book!

I hope this book was able to help you to adopt a minimalist lifestyle.

The next step is to follow the discussed strategies in this book.

Thank you and good luck!

Chloe S

Made in the USA
Coppell, TX
02 June 2022

78395651R10187